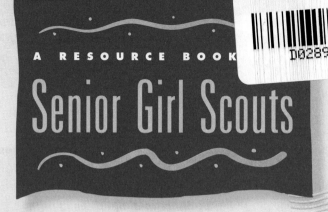

A RESOURCE BOOK

Senior Girl Scouts

Girl Scouts of the U.S.A.

420 Fifth Avenue

New York, N.Y. 10018-2702

GIRL SCOUTS OF THE U.S.A.®

B. LaRae Orullian, *National President*
Mary Rose Main, *National Executive Director*

Project Coordinator
Rosemarie Cryan

Authors
Rosemarie Cryan
Harriet S. Mosatche, Ph.D
Chris Bergerson

Contributors
María L. Cabán
Maria Garcia
Sharon Woods Hussey
Toni Eubanks
Janice Cummings
Marianne Ilaw
Donna Nye
Joan W. Fincutter

Editor
Susan Eno

Designer
Evans Design Associates

Illustrators
Katherine Evans: pages 13, 20, 31,
73, 86, 111, 118, 125
Barbara Haines: cover, pages 14,
38, 39, 146, 147

Photographers
Rick Tango: pages 144, 145
Rex Wilson: pages 13, 20, 31, 73,
86, 99, 111, 118, 125

Inquiries related to *A Resource Book for Senior Girl Scouts* should be directed
to Membership and Program, Girl Scouts of the U.S.A., 420 Fifth Avenue,
New York, N.Y. 10018-2702.

First Impression 1995

Printed in the United States of America

ISBN 0-88441-284-9

10 9 8 7 6 5 4 3

Contents

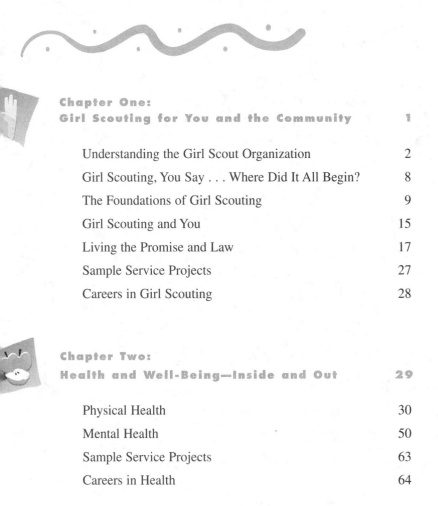

CHAPTER ONE

Girl Scouting for You and the Community

What do leadership, service, sports, science, camping, singing, and careers have in common? Girl Scouting! Being a part of Girl Scouting, the world's largest organization for women and girls, provides you with a wide array of unique opportunities. Through leadership training, interest patches, wider opportunities, career exploration, service projects, spiritual and self-discovery exercises, and a variety of other experiences, Senior Girl Scouts gain a heightened awareness of themselves, their communities, and the world around them.

In surveys conducted by Girl Scouts of the U.S.A., Senior Girl Scouts clearly expressed their interest in serving their communities and preparing for their futures. Each chapter of this handbook, therefore, concludes with a list of service project ideas and careers related to the chapter topics.

Understanding the Girl Scout Organization

Understanding how the overall organization operates will help you to achieve both your long- and short-term goals in Girl Scouting. Basically, Girl Scouting in the United States is comprised of a national organization called Girl Scouts of the U.S.A. (GSUSA) and a countrywide system of councils. Councils are linked to the national organization by charters. Each state has at least one council, and many have more than one.

The Role of Girl Scouts of the U.S.A.

Girl Scouts of the U.S.A. (GSUSA) directs and coordinates the Girl Scout movement in the United States. GSUSA headquarters are located at 420 Fifth Avenue in New York City. Girl Scouts of the U.S.A. depends on the work of volunteers and staff to help support Girl Scouting across the country. Serving a membership of nearly 3.5 million people is a very complex job.

One priority of the national organization is to grant charters to local Girl Scout councils. A charter authorizes a council to make the Girl Scout program available within a designated geographic region. Delegates from each council attend a National Council Session every three years. A volunteer board of directors is elected by the delegates to set national policy. National staff members implement this policy through training, fieldwork, and development of resources.

Away From the World

My common day is bad,
As my days tend to be,
And then I travel home,
To my bizarre family.

I tend to live in my room,
I cry about my ways,
But then I remember,
The day is Thursday.

This changes my mind,
When I want to just pout,
I can't wait until I go,
For tonight is Girl Scouts.

Girl Scouts is the thing,
That lights up my day,
I like to see all my friends,
And hear them yell "Hey!"

We always get excited,
About the things we will do,
We love to just talk,
About books of Who's Who.

I don't want to leave,
When the clock says it's late,
I love it where I am,
To stay is my fate.

But unfortunately it's not,
I get up to leave,
To return to a world,
Where I don't want to be.

It's just a small meeting,
Another day on our chart,
But somehow it seems
Like so much more to my heart.

Angela Twining, 13
Chesapeake Bay
Girl Scout Council,
Delaware

A large number of people are involved in writing handbooks, leaders' guides, and other program materials; supporting wider opportunities with nationwide participation; training girls and adults (council volunteers and staff) at Edith Macy Conference Center; and maintaining membership data files. Many projects are conducted in collaboration with outside agencies such as science museums, national professional associations, and publishing companies.

Each Girl Scout council, which is governed by a board of directors, provides Girl Scout activities within a particular geographic area. Council responsibilities usually include recruitment and training of adult volunteers, and management of the council's resources and facilities such as camps. Professional staff, along with adult Girl Scout volunteers, work to attain goals and objectives set by GSUSA and your council's board of directors.

In addition, many councils sponsor older girl planning boards so that girls from different parts of the council can get together to discuss activities. Some planning boards are organized so that each troop or group sends representatives; others are open to anyone who wants to come. Girls determine how often the group meets, what kinds of events to organize, and where meetings or events are to be held.

Delegate to the National Council of Girl Scouts of the United States of America

As a girl Scout 14 years or older, you are eligible to be a delegate to the National Council, which meets every three years. Delegates, who are elected by their council, serve for three years; they voice their opinions and vote on issues critical to the future of Girl Scouting.

Being a Part of a Worldwide Movement

The Girl Scout Promise and Law (see page 10), along with Girl Scout traditions, unite young women from the United States with girls from abroad. While the activities done by Girl Scouts or Girl Guides in one corner of the

world may differ dramatically from those undertaken by another group in a separate region, Girl Scouts everywhere share common values and a concern for the future.

In 1919, the International Council was formed, later becoming the **World Association of Girl Guides and Girl Scouts (WAGGGS)**. The mission of WAGGGS has always been based on spiritual values, with a commitment to peace and international understanding.

In 1993, there were 128 member organizations, serving over 8.5 million individuals in countries large and small. Each participating nation contributes funds to assure services to all its members. Thinking Day contributions (see pages 11–12) are one of the major sources of WAGGGS income and are used for leadership training, community projects, and international exchanges. Every three years a World Conference is held in a different area of the world and is attended by voting delegates and observers. This conference was held in the United States in 1926, 1948, and 1984.

WAGGGS operates four world centers: Pax Lodge in London, England; Our Chalet in Adelboden, Switzerland; Our Cabaña in Cuernavaca, Mexico; and Sangam in Pune, India. The world centers enable Girl Scouts and

More than 50,000 members and guests from 90 countries have enjoyed happy and rewarding experiences through living and learning together at Our Cabaña.

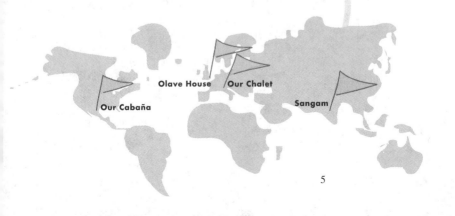

Olave House   Our Chalet

Our Cabaña   Sangam

Girl Guides to experience the culture of the host country, and to interact with and learn about travelers from around the world. All members of the WAGGGS movement may stay at the centers for conferences, seminars, or special holidays. Find out more about these centers from your council office.

Diversity

To be diverse is a wonderful thing
To all sound different in the way we sing;
To all see things in our own separate way
Is what creates an interesting day.

We are diverse, you and I
I am loud, while you are shy;
You have brown eyes; mine are blue,
We are good Friends, me and you.

The reason we are such great Friends
Is because our differences tend to blend;
When I am sad, you make me smile.
And then we'll sit and laugh awhile.

But if we all were just exactly the same,
Both in color and from whence we came;
There would be no cultures to teach each other
For we would all be just like one another.

What fun would it be, to meet someone new
If the person you met was exactly like you;
Be happy with all the difference you bring,
For to be diverse is a wonderful thing.

Joanne Payne, 17
Virginia Skyline
Girl Scout Council,
Virginia

Olave Centre, located in London, houses Pax Lodge (one of the world centers) and the offices of the World Bureau. This complex was built by donations from Girl Scouts and Girl Guides in all regions of the world. The World Bureau directs volunteers and paid staff in achieving the goals of WAGGGS. The Bureau collaborates with the United Nations and its specialized agencies to benefit women and children, and has established a Peace Initiative worldwide.

USA Girl Scouts Overseas

Many Americans spend some time living abroad. Girls whose families have been temporarily transferred to foreign locations can maintain their Girl Scout links by joining American troops or groups in another country. Likewise, girls who have never been Girl Scouts but would like to join when they journey abroad, may also do so.

Young women who are involved in Girl Scouting overseas enjoy a wide array of experiences. Among the various Girl Scout activities are ones designed to further a girl's understanding of the culture of her host country. Some of these are events shared with local Girl Guide/Girl Scout troops, thus promoting awareness that members of both are part of the World Association of Girl Guides and Girl Scouts.

Girl Scouting, You Say . . . Where Did It All Begin?

The story of Girl Scouting really begins with the life of an amazing woman named Juliette Gordon Low. In a time when women were supposed to be domestic, submissive, and passive, Juliette — or Daisy, as she was known to her friends — was a strong woman who was willing to take risks and make things happen. She looked beyond society's usual expectations for women. Daisy appreciated the traditional role of women at home with their families, but she was also eager to use her talents and to explore other, less conventional pursuits. She was an accomplished artist and also wanted to learn about auto mechanics, gardening, and Morse code. She even learned to fly an airplane! Daisy believed that women could do anything, and this belief led to the founding of Girl Scouting in the United States.

Although Daisy Low was a remarkable and talented woman, she was not immune to problems. Daisy suffered from a hearing impairment that left her mostly deaf, but she never let this prevent her from pursuing her interests. She faced personal disappointments as well. She and her husband did not have children. The husband was unfaithful and often cruel. She was on the brink of getting a divorce, something rather uncommon in her time, when her husband died.

The story of Juliette Gordon Low, therefore, offers young women around the world inspiration. Juliette overcame her personal difficulties and created new opportunities for women by acting as a trailblazer and avoiding limiting stereotypes.

The Foundations of Girl Scouting

Girl Scouting is continually evolving to meet the needs of girls. While the activities may change, the fundamental premise and mission of the organization remain the same. These basic principles can be found in the four program goals, the Girl Scout Promise and Law, and the traditions, symbols, and ceremonies associated with Girl Scouting.

The Four Program Goals of Girl Scouting

The goals outlined below influence everything you do in Girl Scouting.

1. Developing to your full individual potential.

2. Relating to others with increasing understanding, skill, and respect.

3. Developing values to guide your actions and to provide the foundation for sound decision-making.

4. Contributing to the improvement of society through the use of your abilities and leadership skills, working in cooperation with others.

Every Girl Scout agrees to live by the Promise and Law.

The Girl Scout Promise

On my honor, I will try:

To serve God and my country,

To help people at all times,

And to live by the Girl Scout Law.

There is a spiritual foundation to the Girl Scout movement. However, since Girl Scouting is for all girls, those whose beliefs may be better expressed by a word or phrase other than "God" may substitute that word or phrase when they say the Girl Scout Promise. When written, the Promise always has the word "God."

The Girl Scout Law

I will do my best:

To be honest

To be fair

To help where I am needed

To be cheerful

To be friendly and considerate

To be a sister to every Girl Scout

To respect authority

To use resources wisely

To protect and improve the world around me

To show respect for myself and others through my words and actions.

The Promise and the Law offer useful guidance for making decisions and can help you to identify personal values that will give meaning and direction to your life.

Girl Scout Symbols, Signs, and Ceremonies

As a part of Girl Scouting you may already know or will learn about a number of traditions, symbols, and signs that have been passed from generation to generation of Girl Scouts.

Friendship circle: Everyone stands in a circle and each person crosses her right arm over her left, clasping hands with her friends on both sides.

Friendship squeeze: As everyone stands silently in the friendship circle, a squeeze is passed from hand to hand.

Girl Scout handshake: A form of greeting used by Girl Scouts and Girl Guides all around the world. It is done by shaking hands with the left hand while making the Girl Scout sign with the right. The left hand is the one nearest the heart and therefore signifies friendship.

Girl Scout sign: A form of greeting exchanged whenever Girl Scouts and Girl Guides meet. Three fingers of the right hand are extended to symbolize the three parts of the Promise.

Girl Scout motto: "Be prepared."

Girl Scout slogan: "Do a good turn daily."

Thinking Day (February 22): This is the birthday of both Robert, Lord Baden-Powell, who founded the Boy Scout movement in England, and his wife, Olave, Lady

Baden-Powell, who was the World Chief Guide of the Girl Guide/Girl Scout movement. Girl Guides and Girl Scouts make a special effort to meet on Thinking Day to exchange greetings with their sisters in other countries and to give contributions to the Thinking Day Fund. This fund is used to promote the Girl Guide/Girl Scout movement throughout the world and to help Girl Guide and Girl Scout organizations in various countries.

Following are some common Girl Scout ceremonies:

- **_Investiture ceremony._** Is held to welcome someone into Girl Scouting for the first time.

- **_Bridging ceremony._** Is held when you "cross the bridge" to the next level in Girl Scouting.

- **_Rededication ceremony._** Is held at special times when Girl Scouts want to renew their Girl Scout Promise and review what the Girl Scout Law means to them. Troops usually hold one at the beginning of each troop year. A Girl Scout member can take part in many rededication ceremonies.

- **_Court of Awards ceremony._** Is an occasion at which girls receive recognitions that they have earned.

- **_Girl Scouts' Own ceremony._** Is a special ceremony created by a troop or group around a theme.

- **_Indoor flag ceremony._** This ceremony has the following steps:

  1. The troop/group forms a horseshoe. The color guard is in position. All stand at attention.

2. The Girl Scout-in-charge says: "Color guard, advance." This signals the color guard to advance to the flags, salute the American flag, and pick the flags up. Then they turn together and get into position facing the troop. Everyone stands at attention.

3. The color guard walks forward carrying the flags to the formation. They stop in front of the flags.

4. The Girl Scout-in-charge says: "Girl Scouts, honor the flag of your country." The group salutes the American flag.

5. The Girl Scout-in-charge says: "Girl Scouts, recite the Pledge of Allegiance." This may be followed by songs, poems, or verses.

6. The Girl Scout-in-charge says: "Color guard, post the colors." This signals the color bearers to place the flags in their stands. They remain at attention next to the flags. If the flag ceremony is a part of a larger ceremony such as an investiture, the Girl Scout-in-charge commands the color guard to retire the colors by taking the flags to their place of storage. The following commands can be used:

"Girl Scouts, attention."

"Color guard, advance."

"Color guard, honor your flag."

"Color guard, retire the colors."

"Color guard, dismissed."

"Girl Scouts, dismissed."

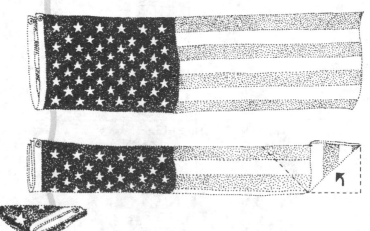

How to fold the flag

Girl Scouting and You

Fitting Girl Scouting into your life is not always easy, but the Girl Scout program is purposely flexible to meet a variety of needs and lifestyles. What are your reasons for being a Girl Scout? Much of what you learn and do in Girl Scouting will help you in other areas of your life — school, home, friends, work, community, religion — and the skills you gain from participating in these institutions can help you in your Girl Scout endeavors.

Girl Scouts

Girl Scouts
Camping out
Campfires
Cookie buyers
Having fun
Get things done
Singing songs
Banging gongs
Meetings
Greetings
Different places
Friendly faces
Taking trips
Seeing ships
Eating chips
Making crafts
Laughing laughs
Swimming laps
Singing taps
All this stuff...can't you see
That's what Girl Scouts
means to me

Cara Tirone, 14
Plymouth Bay
Girl Scout Council,
Massachusetts

As a Senior Girl Scout, you have opportunities to share your knowledge and experience with younger girls. You might lead an activity for Daisy or Brownie Girl Scouts, or you could intrigue Junior Girl Scouts with stories about a trip that you have been on. Take advantage of the many formal opportunities for leadership with younger girls, such as being a Senior Girl Scout Program Aide, Leader-in-Training (LIT), or Counselor-in-Training (CIT) (see pages 72–74). There are also many informal opportunities where you may find yourself interacting with younger girls, and suddenly you are a role model!

FAMOUS FORMER GIRL SCOUTS

Carol Moseley Braun *(attorney and U.S. Senator)*

Hillary Rodham Clinton *(attorney and First Lady)*

Katie Couric *(co-host of the* Today Show*)*

Dr. Millie Hughes-Fulford *(former astronaut, research scientist)*

Tamara Jernigan *(astronaut)*

Jackie Joyner-Kersee *(Olympic track and field gold medalist)*

Nancy Lopez *(professional golfer)*

Barbara Mikulski *(U.S. Senator)*

Sandra Day O'Connor *(U.S. Supreme Court Justice)*

Chita Rivera *(actress)*

Gloria Steinem *(writer)*

Vicki Van Meter *(youngest girl to pilot cross-country)*

Judith Viorst *(writer)*

Can you add some names from your community?

Living the Promise and Law

Your values include those things that are most important to you — perhaps friendship, money, and helping others. Ethical values are specifically related to your sense of morality — your notion of right and wrong. Many meaningful decisions that you make in life come from a set of ethical values that you have been formulating since you were young. These values are influenced by your family, religious and spiritual teachings, your ethnic and racial heritage, your education, Girl Scouting, your peers, your community, and the world around you.

The Girl Scout program is based on a set of basic ethical values. These values include a concern for others, honesty, fairness, citizenship, responsibility, and respect for differences. When making personal and group decisions, these ethical values can be helpful. The model described below can guide you in resolving ethical dilemmas.

1. Define your problem. Whom does it affect? Do you need any additional information?

2. What values play a part in the dilemma? What moral principles and beliefs (honesty and fairness, for example) should guide your actions?

3. List all possible solutions.

4. Look at the way your solutions mesh with your ethical values. Is there a major conflict? Is someone going to get hurt by the action? Is it really unfair? Is it dishonest? Is it against the law? Does it make you feel guilty?

   • If a conflict exists, can you change something that would make the circumstances fit comfortably with your ethical values? If not, eliminate this as a possible solution.

   • If your values and solutions work together, rank the possible solutions in order of preference and in order of good created for others and yourself.

5. Assess the solution. How do you feel about your choice? Do you need to do some adjusting? How would your friends react? How about your family? Do you need to ask other people you respect?

6. Take action. Make your decision based upon your ethical values and your evaluation of the problem.

7. Evaluate. Are you comfortable with your decision? Will you do it the same way next time?

The situations below are ones that you may encounter either now or in the future. Think about how you would react and the criteria upon which you would base your decisions.

• Cheating on your income tax?

• Getting out of jury duty because it's not convenient?

• Driving after drinking alcohol?

There is a clear relationship between alcohol and grade-point average. In general, people who receive D's and F's drink more than those who receive A's.

- Supporting a decision to pull a life-support system from a dying relative?

- Lying if asked to do so by your boss?

- Fighting in a war?

- Smoking?

- Ending a pregnancy?

Take one or more of the situations and think it through by listing the factors that contribute to your decision. Discuss these situations with friends or family members. Find out how they would resolve the dilemmas.

Dilemmas in Decision-Making

Stephanie: *I'm president of the environmental club, and my aunt just gave me a beautiful fur-trimmed ski jacket. It looks great. Should I wear it? What do you guys think?*

Latisha: *Well, I know my aunt would just die if I didn't wear a jacket that she gave me. I know she has to work really hard to earn money for the gifts that she gives to me, and I really love her for it. After all, how would you feel if somebody returned your gift?*

Natalie: *I could never wear a fur-trimmed ski jacket, no matter who gave it to me. An animal was killed to make that jacket. If I wore it, I would be going against my beliefs and against the principles of the environmental club.*

Carmen: *I'm not sure what I'd do. I really think it's important to practice what you preach, and I really believe in taking care of the earth, but I think people's feelings are important too. That's really quite a dilemma!*

Many decisions involve complex issues, and sometimes there is not enough time to analyze each of them. What may have seemed a simple yes-or-no decision to you when you were younger has now become a multifaceted problem. Decisions are not always questions of "right versus wrong." They can be questions of "right versus right," or even "wrong versus wrong." The dilemma

comes from trying to make the best choice between two actions that could both be right, or getting overwhelmed because no solution is immediately apparent to you.

In theory, a situation shouldn't present a dilemma for you if one of the choices goes against your ethical values, because it is assumed that you would always choose to do the "right" thing. However, in real life, ethical decision-making is not always easy. Sometimes it takes practice, and often it takes courage.

Getting the Opinions of Others

Talk with adults whom you respect. Ask them about difficult decisions that they have faced. Ask them how they made those decisions. Ask each about the biggest lesson she or he learned from making a wrong decision.

Sometimes, actions that go against your basic values can be hard to live with. Walking by the homeless person who is asking for food, or lying to your mother about where you're going can cause guilt, which results from the incompatibility of your actions and your principles. On the next page are some more situations to consider. Read them and decide how you would act. Compare your answer with someone else's answer. Did you both arrive at the same conclusion? What was your reasoning? Did the other person use different reasoning? Were there any clear-cut decisions?

- My track coach wants me to run every night after school so that I can win for our school. My dad just got laid off work and I was offered a job at the mall. Our family could use the money.

- I was assigned a lab partner at school who doesn't speak English very well and dresses differently because of her religion. She is very good in science and is a really nice person. My friends have been making fun of her. She has invited me over to her house for dinner. Should I go? Should I tell my friends?

- My next-door neighbor has been in a special ed class in another school for years. Now he has been transferred to my school. My parents want me to ride the bus with him and to show him around school. Will I have to spend all my time with him?

Thinking critically and being able to analyze your options in difficult or tense situations are important skills to have. As you consider each of the above dilemmas, you will gain more insights into your own decision-making strategies.

Taking Action

As a Girl Scout you have many opportunities to serve your community. Many young women undertake challenging and gratifying projects that make significant contributions to the people and places around them. The planning process on the next page can serve as a guide when developing or implementing a project.

Designing Community Service Projects

Identify a problem
- Consult with community leaders.
- Draw on your personal experiences or interests.
- Brainstorm with friends.

Collect information
- Decide what you could do to help.
- Find out about costs and other necessary resources.
- Check out available community support.

Brainstorm actions, directions, or solutions

Make concrete plans
- Check Girl Scout health and safety standards.
- Consider the attitudes and skills of the participants.
- Anticipate hurdles or problems.
- Establish time lines.
- Work with adults but make sure your thinking and work are part of the plan.
- If you are working with younger girls, find out whether the project is realistic for their age level.

Work on your project

Evaluate the project

Share your project successes and challenges with others

In designing a community service project, it is important to follow the policies described in *Safety-Wise*. Generally, you can help an organization or special cause with a service project. For example, you might consider assisting with first aid at a charity walk-a-thon.

But you are not supposed to ask people for money to raise funds for other organizations if you are working as a Girl Scout. As a Girl Scout you can help to register voters, but you shouldn't campaign for a political candidate. Projects that address sensitive issues in your community need to be approved by your Girl Scout council before you make any commitments.

Community service does not end with Girl Scouting. You will have opportunities through school, through religious affiliations, and as an individual to give service or raise money for actions that you support.

Addressing Contemporary and Sensitive Issues
The GSUSA Contemporary Issues series for leaders addresses topics (such as substance abuse, family crises, and prejudice) that are of concern to girls of all ages. You may choose to use the Contemporary Issues booklets to explore subjects within the troop or group setting. Through your Girl Scout council, you can also request special training in sensitive issues to become eligible to work with younger girls on contemporary issues. As an individual, you may decide to become active in areas of personal interest, supporting organizations through service or donations.

The Contemporary Issues series is comprised of 11 publications.

Here are some things you can do as a Girl Scout to address contemporary issues:

- Sponsor a wellness fair.

- Learn about different self-defense techniques and then teach them to others.

- Start a student coalition at school to address important issues, such as drunk driving or substance abuse.

- Set up a peer counseling program.

- Start a literacy program for immigrants.

- Volunteer at an AIDS clinic, a soup kitchen, a women's shelter, or a suicide prevention hotline.

- Organize a panel discussion for parents and teens to promote understanding or resolve conflict.

- Set up a career fair for science and math using women mentors.

- Start a recycling program.

- Work with younger girls to help them prevent or avoid abuse.

- Start an environmental club at school.

- Honor women who have contributed to your community.

- Organize an event to make people aware of gender bias.

Grow to your fullest potential.

Initiate positive change.

Respect differences among people.

Lead others in a variety of endeavors.

Share your experiences with younger girls.

Care for the environment.

Open doors to the future.

Undertake challenges and surpass expectations.

Travel the world through international events.

Show how Girl Scouting enriches your life.

Sample Service Projects

- Create a multicultural, multiracial group to combat racism in your community. Sponsor community activities and training to bring teens together.

- Work at a soup kitchen or food distribution center for people who need assistance.

- Do something for Thinking Day for someone in another country in partnership with WAGGGS, the United Nations, or a global helping organization, such as sending schoolbooks and supplies to children who need them.

- Help collect used clothing for a community shelter for the homeless.

- Volunteer in a literacy program by tutoring or reading with young children.

- Help organize an Earth Day (April 22) celebration. Invite environmental groups to attend, create a list of community projects to accomplish, and get people to sign up.

- Put together a resource center dealing with nature. With help from your council, develop a "wish list" for resource books, equipment, and maintenance, and get people to commit to making the wishes come true. Bring everyone together to work, and celebrate with a "housewarming" for the center.

- Do an energy survey at a council-owned property, school, or home. Make plans to reduce energy and resource consumption by 10 percent.

- Develop a wildlife feeding area at a camp or park by planting native forage for wildlife and birds.

Careers in Girl Scouting

Land use planner

Program and membership specialist

Compensation analyst

Executive director

Public relations specialist

Adult development director

Director of program services

Director of fund development

Field director

Ranger

Product sales specialist

Resident camp director

Younger girl program specialist

Assistant executive director

Director of program events

CHAPTER TWO

Health and Well-Being — Inside and Out

Fat-free food, mineral water, diet manuals, and pamphlets entitled "How to Have Happy Relationships in Three Easy Steps" and "How to Avoid AIDS" are a few of the many items that might be placed in a "time capsule" dedicated to describing health in the 1990s. People today are reevaluating the definition of well-being. Health no longer means simply the absence of disease but instead now refers to one's entire physical, emotional, and psychological state.

As a young child, you were probably not as conscious of your health or of your psychological state as you are today. Sickness probably meant a day home from school and more television than you were normally allowed to watch. Similarly, your emotions were probably much more identifiable — anger at not being allowed to get a toy that you wanted, happiness that you could have your best friend sleep over, sadness that summer camp was ending.

Today, you may find that you are aware of a much wider spectrum of emotions. Perhaps you sometimes feel depressed or worried or elated or giddy for no particular *reason. These emotions may be directly related to hormonal or physical changes, or they may derive from your relationships with the other people around you.*

Maintaining a healthy state of mind and body requires a conscious effort on your part. The attitudes and routines that you develop as a teenager will affect your health and happiness as an adult.

Physical Health

In some ways, women are particularly fortunate when it comes to their physical health. A number of unique characteristics are associated with the female body. For example, did you know that . . .

• Women have a greater peripheral vision and are able to see better in the dark than men.

• Women have better balance than men as a result of their narrower shoulders and wider hips.

• Women bear physical pain better than men.

• Women hear better than men.

• Women get fewer viral and bacterial illnesses than men.

• Women are more flexible and limber than men.

Although women should be proud of their bodies and aware of their special characteristics, they should not take good health for granted. In fact, certain physical health concerns are particularly relevant for women. Eating disorders, premenstrual syndrome, and breast cancer are a few examples. Teenage women in American society must also contend with issues like AIDS and substance abuse.

Special Health Concerns for Women

Anorexia Nervosa

Anorexia nervosa is a disease in which a person has an overwhelming desire to be thin and a tremendous fear of being fat. Because of a very unrealistic self-image, she will often starve herself to the point of weighing less than two-thirds of what is considered normal for her height and build.

Despite her tremendous weight loss, the anorexic is unable to recognize how thin she is or that she needs help. Her skin can become blotchy and she may develop fine, soft hair all over her body. She may develop low body temperature, a low heart rate, and low blood pressure, and her menstrual periods may stop.

Frequently, women who suffer from this disease were heavy in the past and are obsessed about regaining the weight. They impose very strict controls over what they eat until they eat almost nothing. Excessive exercise, laxatives, diuretics, and self-induced vomiting are other techniques used to control weight. Some experts believe that anorexia is an attempt on the part of young women

It Won't Matter in the End

Waking up each morning
Looking in the mirror
With a face of disgust
At her reflection
A bit too much here
Way too much there

At breakfast she just picks at her food
Thinking of the consequences of eating it
But longing for a nibble
Using restraint
She refuses the food
During the day
She is weak and dizzy
She hears her body crying
For food
Wanting to eat too
But she is still too fat

Her friends tell her
She has the perfect body
But she ignores them
Just as she ignores the calls of her body
At home her parents have no clue
Exactly what she is going through
They ask her if she ate
And every single time
She tells them she will later

On television that night
She sees a model who weighs all of
120 pounds
Longing to be like her
But she hears her stomach call
So she gives in and
Eats only 3 crackers
And drinks nothing but water

to return to the safety of childhood and avoid the problems of growing up. Others suggest that starvation offers young women who don't feel in control of their lives a way of exercising control over themselves and those around them.

Treatment usually consists of a combination of psychological counseling and a high-calorie diet. Recovery depends on how long a person has been anorexic. Receiving early professional help for this condition is important. The outlook for long-term anorexics is not very good. Anorexic women are thought to be at a higher risk for developing osteoporosis (see page 40) at an early age, and can develop a life-threatening heart condition.

After she had eaten that "huge" meal
She thinks she ate too much
And walks into the bathroom
Although it is painful
She still goes through
The ritual of
Leaning over the toilet
And sticking her finger down her throat

Every day she is getting thinner
Her clothes are getting bigger
She starts to notice the change in her figure
Her friends start to worry
And her parents likewise
But she continues the daily routine
Of watching everything she eats
Soon she is way under
120 pounds
87 pounds to be exact

Still not thin enough
She throws up for the last time
For her body can't take
Anymore of the starvation
She passes out on the bathroom floor
And the next day she is no more

Six feet under the ground
She is now
With no one to notice
How thin she is

> *Jameika Sampson, 14*
> *Great Rivers*
> *Girl Scout Council,*
> *Ohio*

Bulimia

People with bulimia alternate between binge eating and self-induced vomiting to control weight gain. Some bulimics abuse diuretics and laxatives, go on fasts, or exercise all the time.

You may not know if someone is bulimic by looking at her; she may appear healthy, with a body weight normal for her age and size. Because of this, even her family may not know that she has an eating disorder.

Estimates of bulimia among young women in high school and college range from 5 to 30 percent. As with anorexia, most sufferers are females. All kinds of physical problems can develop from constant bingeing and vomiting, such as inflammation of the esophagus, kidney trouble, rotting teeth, abnormal heart rhythms, and paralysis.

Psychological therapy is very important in altering the obsessive behavior of bulimic sufferers toward food. Keeping a diary of what the person eats and the things that make her resort to bingeing is one technique that has been successful in reversing this destructive behavior.

One-fifth of high school girls have used diet pills, more than one in six have forced themselves to vomit, and half have skipped a meal in order to lose weight.

Premenstrual Syndrome

Feeling particularly tired, cranky, or bloated? Maybe your period is due to begin. Many women experience a variety of symptoms that signal the onset of their menstrual periods. These cues can be both physical and emotional.

On the days that precede your period, you may experience intense mood swings, feeling alternately happy and sad with little or no provocation. Some women feel unnaturally depressed as a result of premenstrual syndrome. If you are aware that these feelings are being triggered by the hormonal reactions that menstruation causes, you will be better able to deal with them.

In the days prior to your period, try to reduce your feelings of stress or depression by doing the things that you enjoy. Review the list on page 61 for some ideas about activities that relieve stress. Also, do not stop engaging in physical activity or attending sports practices or games just because you think that your period might begin. In fact, physical activity might be just what you need, both mentally and physically. If you are subject to intense cramps or serious discomfort prior to your period, talk to your physician. Some prescription medications are available that can help alleviate premenstrual pain.

Breast Cancer

Not too long ago, you were acutely aware of the physical changes your body was undergoing as you began that exciting and sometimes frightening journey from childhood to womanhood. You may have felt self-conscious about your blossoming femininity because of the extra attention or teasing by boys. On the other hand, you may have been delighted about your changing body and excited about being on the threshold of new adventures. In either case, because you were undergoing such an amazing metamorphosis, you were very aware of how your body looked and felt. With time, you became comfortable with the "new" you.

Even though you know that keeping healthy is important, you probably pay more attention to parts of your body — ears, hands, teeth — that help you "do" something. Healthy breasts are just as important to your overall well-being as any other part of your body.

Although pain is a good indicator that something is wrong, don't rely on this when breasts are concerned. Most breast cancers in the United States are discovered by touch, either by accident or by examination by a woman or her doctor. Self-examination and mammography (special X-rays of the breast) are the two major methods of detecting cancers early. While you need a medical professional for an X-ray, you can easily examine yourself by following the steps outlined on pages 38 and 39.

Most breast irregularities are found by women themselves. Yet many women do not know how to perform breast self-examinations and few do so regularly.

It is best to examine your breasts once a month. In this way, you will become accustomed to what feels normal for you. Breast tissue is made up of small lobes, ducts, nourishing fluid, tissue, and fat. Do an exam about four to seven days after the end of each period; before then, your breasts might be a little lumpy due to normal swelling of the ducts and tissue. If you don't have regular periods, examine your breasts on the first day of each month. Become familiar with how your breasts normally feel so you can pick up any changes that occur.

Here is what you should look for:

• A lump, lumpy area, or thickening.

• Swelling, bulging, puckering, or dimpling of the skin and the breast.

• Drawing back or turning in of the nipple.

• A discharge, clear or bloody, from the nipple.

• A rash on the nipple.

• Swelling of the upper arm.

• Enlarged glands under the arm.

Breast Self-Examination

Step 1

While in the shower, place your right arm behind your head and glide your left hand, fingers flat, over your entire right breast. Press gently, using small circular motions, and feel around your entire breast while tracing circles around it from the outside to the nipple. Reverse for the left breast.

Step 2

Standing in front of a mirror, put your hands behind your head and check the front and both sides of your breasts. Tighten your chest muscles by placing your hands on your hips and moving your shoulders up and down. Check the front and back of both breasts again.

Step 1

Step 2

Step 3

While lying down, place a pillow under your right shoulder and put your right hand behind your head. With the fingers of the left hand, repeat Step 1. Feel under your armpit and your upper chest, too. Reverse for the left breast.

Step 4

Check the color and condition of your nipples. Gently squeeze each one to check if there is a discharge (this can signal a problem).

Don't panic if you feel lumps or see something unusual; breast cancer is rare in young women. If you have concerns, discuss them immediately with a parent, guardian, or other adult you trust and your doctor.

Step 3

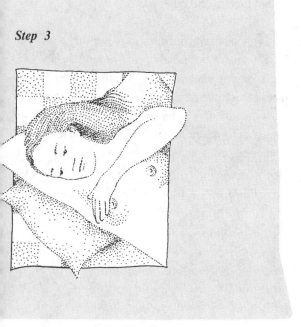

Osteoporosis

Have you ever seen an elderly woman hunched over and unable to straighten to her full height? Sometimes this deformity is a result of an ailment called osteoporosis. Osteoporosis is a medical condition associated with loss of bone mass and is most often found in women.

Lack of calcium contributes to loss of bone mass, one of the major causes of osteoporosis.

Although osteoporosis generally occurs in women after menopause, usually age 50 or more, it is important for teenage girls to be aware of this illness because a proper diet and exercise routine now can strengthen muscles and bones and help make you less susceptible. Calcium is an important nutrient that strengthens bones. Lack of calcium can contribute to the loss of bone mass, one of the major causes of osteoporosis. Milk and other dairy products, including cheese, yogurt, and ice cream, have a high calcium content. You can also get calcium in sardines, broccoli, collard greens, and other foods.

Exercise is another critical factor in preventing osteoporosis. A woman's bone mass peaks around the age of 35. Weight-bearing exercises, like walking, running, or any other activity that requires your bones to sustain a significant amount of weight, increase bone density. By exercising as a teenager, therefore, you can make your bones as strong and dense as possible. Then, when bone loss naturally occurs in later years, it may be less likely to lead to osteoporosis.

Acquired Immune Deficiency Syndrome (AIDS)

Acquired Immune Deficiency Syndrome (AIDS) is a viral disease that weakens the immune system. A weakened immune system restricts the body's ability to fight deadly infections. Therefore, people who contract AIDS end up suffering from any number of fatal diseases, including several forms of cancer. The HIV (human immunodeficiency virus) is believed to be the main cause of AIDS. A person infected with HIV, but who has not yet developed AIDS, is referred to as being HIV-positive. It has not yet been proven that everybody infected with HIV will develop AIDS, but the likelihood is that they will.

AIDS has not and will not go peacefully away. There is still no cure for it. This means that on the basis of knowledge we have now, if you contract AIDS, you will eventually die from it. You should take the threat of AIDS very seriously, even if you think you are not likely to get it. AIDS is the sixth leading cause of death among people ages 15 to 24.

In connection with AIDS, reference is often made to "risky" or "unsafe" behavior. The two most risky behaviors are having unprotected sex and sharing intravenous needles, though people should also be careful of needles used in tattooing or ear-piercing. Behaviors that allow for the exchange of body fluids can also provide a means for AIDS to enter the body.

AIDS is the sixth leading cause of death among people ages 15 - 24.

The National AIDS hotline number is 1-800-342-AIDS.

One-fourth of all adolescents contract a sexually transmitted disease before graduating from high school.

Parents, teachers, and religious leaders in the community, as well as young people themselves, are all concerned about the spread of AIDS through risky behaviors. Peer pressure becomes a risk factor when you feel you must behave according to a group expectation. Drinking alcohol is a risk factor because it can cause you to lower your guard and loosen normal inhibitions. Those two conditions can lead to unplanned, unprotected sex — a very serious risk factor for AIDS.

Just how much at risk are you for the AIDS virus if nobody you know practices risky behavior? First of all, how do you know the people you interact with have not participated in activities that put them at risk for contracting the AIDS virus?

A boy is at a party where everybody is "doing drugs." Out of either pressure from the group, or curiosity, he tries the drug for "just that one time," not knowing that he's using a lethal needle. Tainted blood on an intravenous needle is not necessarily visible.

By the time you meet this boy, he could present himself to you as the most wholesome, clean, well-dressed, popular boy in school — and he could be from the most respected family in the community. But he could be carrying the AIDS virus and not yet know it.

More than 85 percent of Americans have not been tested for the AIDS virus, although this would be a significant way to stop the spread of the disease. Many people, especially young people, do not avail themselves of testing at clinics and doctors' offices. They may be frightened, may feel a stigma attached to being tested, or may feel that it is an acknowledgment of their risky behavior. This is unfortunate because of the rapidly increasing heterosexual transmission of AIDS. Women are almost 18 times more likely to be infected in heterosexual behavior than men, and they die at twice the rate of men with the same diagnosis.

How can you protect yourself? Abstinence from sexual intercourse and drug use is the most effective method of protection against the AIDS virus.

You can donate blood without any fear of contracting AIDS, and since the nation's blood supply has been screened, it is now safer to have a blood transfusion. You can't get AIDS from towels, food, toilet seats, hugging, kissing, or befriending a person with AIDS. Consult with health care professionals or other groups that offer in-depth advice on AIDS prevention. You might even sponsor an awareness forum with your friends. For answers to questions, call the National AIDS Hotline at 1-800-342-AIDS.

Alcohol Abuse

A champagne toast for the bride and groom; a wine and cheese reception following a classical music recital; beer and pretzels during a football game — in many cultures, alcohol is used to celebrate milestones or make social events special. But some people use alcohol to escape everyday problems, to conquer fears or feelings of inadequacy, or to overcome boredom. Because growing up is a

The average person can metabolize about 12 ounces of beer, 4 ounces of wine, or a 1-ounce shot of whiskey or vodka per hour.

process of finding out who you are, where you belong, and testing limits, some adolescents also use alcohol just to try something new, to rebel against parents, or to be thought of as cool.

The physical effects of alcohol are important. No matter what the quantity, alcohol is absorbed directly into your bloodstream and circulates throughout your body within minutes. Alcohol enters your body quickly, but takes a while to leave your system because the liver can only burn about 12 ounces of beer, 4 ounces of wine, or a 1-ounce shot of whiskey or vodka per hour.

Alcohol is classified as a drug that depresses the central nervous system and can cause addiction if abused. Coordination, reflexes, and behavior may all be affected. Long-term abusers of alcohol can develop malnutrition, ulcers, liver damage, heart disease, brain and nerve damage, and delirium tremens or "DTs" (violent tremors, memory loss, and hallucinations).

Women are more affected by alcohol because of their metabolism and body structure. Because of this, women suffer liver damage earlier than men after drinking less during shorter periods of time. This also means that a woman who has had the same amount to drink as a man will show higher levels of blood alcohol and therefore will be more vulnerable to experiencing problems of coordination, such as that demanded by driving.

Approximately two out of five people in the United States will be in an alcohol-related car crash in their lifetime.

Alcohol affects women in another important way: it can cause damage to an unborn child. A woman doesn't have to be a hard drinker for alcohol to have a toxic effect on her fetus; even small quantities of alcohol during pregnancy can lead to fetal damage. Doctors are not sure how much alcohol it takes to cause damage in the unborn child, so the best thing a woman can do is not drink any alcohol while she is pregnant or suspects she may be pregnant.

Here are some tips for minimizing potentially dangerous situations involving alcohol:

- Find out ahead of time how new acquaintances are likely to behave in a social setting.

- Always carry extra cash to pay for cab fare home in case things get out of hand and a parent or friend can't pick you up.

- Know who can be an emergency backup if the person on whom you were depending for a ride cannot follow through on her or his commitment.

- Don't involve yourself in drinking contests or eat alcohol-laced gelatin cubes. Rapid consumption of alcohol can cause poisoning and even death.

- The combination of drugs, even over-the-counter medication, and alcohol can be extremely dangerous. People with disabilities or health impairments that require medication are extremely susceptible to this problem.

FRIENDS DON'T LET
FRIENDS DRIVE DRUNK

Cigarette Smoking

When you hear the word "addict" you probably think of someone who is hooked on drugs or alcohol, but smokers are addicts too. Nicotine is a drug, and smoking is the largest addiction problem in the United States. The problem is, smokers develop a tolerance for nicotine, so they need to smoke more to get the same effect, which ultimately results in a dependency on this drug.

While paid advertising from the tobacco industry in magazines, on billboards, and in movies may make smoking seem glamorous, this habit has many harmful effects. For example, smoking can cause lung cancer, emphysema, and heart disease. It can also raise blood pressure and cause women to give birth to smaller babies.

The tobacco industry spends nearly $4 billion annually, or $11 million dollars a day, to advertise and promote cigarettes.

While most Americans are placing more and more restrictions on smoking, the numbers of teenage girls who smoke are on the rise. What can you do to get the message out?

Drug Abuse

People take drugs for a variety of reasons — pressure and influence from peers; rebellion against parents, teachers, and others in positions of authority; tension at home or at school; to satisfy curiosity; to relieve boredom, depression, or anxiety; for relaxation or pleasure. Using drugs, however, creates a paradox for many teenagers. In the short term, taking drugs can relieve certain stresses by creating an artificial "high." In fact, while the chemicals are running through the bloodstream, drugs can make an individual feel powerful or invincible and much better equipped to deal with life's challenges. When the effects of the drug wear off, however, the user is in danger of plummeting to even lower mood levels, leaving her feeling profoundly depressed, upset, or embarrassed. In addition, habitual use of drugs will impair your ability to perform your routine functions. In school, on the athletic field, or in any of your activities, you will be at a disadvantage both physically and emotionally if you have come to rely on drugs.

You can do a number of things to educate your friends and community about the harmful effects of using drugs. You might create a "wellness fair" as described on pages 48-49, being sure to invite an expert in the field of substance abuse. Or, attend leadership training so that you can teach younger girls about the effects of alcohol, cigarettes, and drugs.

Automobile Accidents

Research indicates that adolescents are particularly likely to be involved in automobile accidents. There are many explanations for this phenomenon, including: teenagers are new drivers; adolescents may combine drinking and driving; and young drivers are more willing to take risks, not imagining that they could be seriously hurt or die.

Involvement in an accident can be very traumatic. Talk to your parents/guardians about what to do if an accident occurs. Things you may want to discuss include: who will call the insurance company, what information is needed from the other driver, how to fill out an insurance accident report, how to read a driver's license (which one really is the license number?), and how to contact the police. It will also be helpful to keep two lists of emergency telephone numbers, one in the vehicle and the other in your wallet.

Insurance companies will provide individuals with a booklet or kit on what to do if involved in a motor vehicle accident. If you're involved in an accident, use that kit to help you gather information. Often a diagram is provided that allows you to draw in positions of vehicles, cross streets, stoplights, other vehicles, and so on. A general description of what happened and other information will usually be requested.

Girl Scout Activities

There are many ways that you can use your knowledge of pressing health issues to educate others in your community. Try the suggestions listed below, or think of others that might be appropriate for your troop or group based on your interests and the time available.

Host a "Wellness Fair"

Create a day-long event dedicated to special health concerns for women. Use the information and issues in this chapter as a springboard for developing this event. Talk to doctors and other health professionals about breast cancer, osteoporosis, and eating disorders. You may want to arrange a panel discussion based on these and other relevant topics. Perhaps you would like to set up booths where you can provide information and pamphlets on different health concerns.

You may want to combine aspects of physical fitness in your program. Maybe a trainer from a local gym could speak either formally or informally to the participants at your fair. Perhaps you would like someone to talk about the benefits of aerobic exercise. Gym teachers and certified aerobics instructors would be good sources.

No matter what format your "wellness fair" takes, you will be providing your community with a valuable service because the more knowledge people have, the better equipped they will be to live healthy lifestyles. Make sure, however, that you are presenting accurate facts on any issue that you address at your event.

Sponsor a Health Career Symposium
With increasingly sophisticated medical technology and longer life expectancies, careers in health care are ever expanding. Together with your troop or with other Girl Scouts from your council, create a health career symposium. Invite experts from a variety of disciplines to participate in a panel discussion or to share their experiences in a short talk or presentation. You will be pleasantly surprised about how willing many professionals are to talk about their jobs and to describe how one might enter into a particular field.

Educate Younger Girls About Health Issues

Write a play about an issue such as drugs or alcoholism that you can share with Brownie or Junior Girl Scouts. Help them to see the ramifications of different choices and lifestyles. Present your play in a way that serves to educate the youngsters without scaring them. Make sure that the facts in your play are correct. You can ask a medical professional to read your script to check for accuracy.

Mental Health

To be healthy, people must be not only physically fit but mentally fit as well. A sense of psychological well-being involves social and emotional components. Interaction among people is an inherent part of life and is, at times, both exciting and stressful. Dating, peer pressure, and family dynamics are a few of the many factors that may cause tension in your personal life. Sexuality, too, is an area that is closely linked to relationships and frequently causes confusion in the lives of teenagers.

Self-Image: Who Decides What You Should Look Like?

Today's ideal woman is independent, assertive, and works — inside and/or outside of the home. Even though she may be a successful homemaker or businesswoman, advertisers still tell her that she will not reach her true

Inner Beauty

Don't judge me by my appearance
My treasures are held within
Behold what you might find
And discover what I may send
Absorb my knowledge and hold my beauty
To create a ring of gold
Pleased to quench your desire
To discover what my mind beholds

> *Shaunda M. Betts, 17*
> *San Jacinto Girl Scouts,*
> *Texas*

potential until she attains a certain physical appearance: beautiful, tall, thin, and young. There is a problem with this portrait — it isn't real. The pearly white teeth, glossy curls, perfect skin, and fantastic figures of models in print ads many times are due more to the magic of air-brush, computer enhancement, and surgery than to genetics or balanced diet.

Although you enjoy looking your best, it would be demeaning if someone judged you solely on the basis of your physical appearance. After all, your intelligence, kindness, abilities, and dreams cannot be determined by how large a bust you have or the size of your clothes. So why do many women strive to achieve someone else's standards?

The images that you see in print, on TV, and in movies send powerful messages. Most people want to look their best. This can be hard to achieve if looking one's best means achieving the perfection created in ads and media images. Even many supermodels aren't "perfect" enough; photos of them are enhanced by computer retouching. Comparing oneself to an unrealistic image of the ultimate woman can result in a negative body image and may lead to the development of eating disorders, such as the ones described on pages 31-34.

Still, many women are not affected in this way by the media. The difference lies in their high self-esteem. If you believe in your self-worth, you'll feel comfortable expressing your individuality without regard to what others may say.

Dating and Relationships

Dilemmas Posed by Dating

Next Saturday is your best friend Mayuko's sixteenth birthday, and you've planned a special surprise: front-row tickets to the home team's basketball game, followed by a pizza party with five of your best girlfriends. But now, you have a dilemma: Your boyfriend informs you that his distant cousin, who stars in your favorite soap opera, will be visiting from California on

Saturday afternoon. It's a once-in-a-lifetime opportunity to meet one of your idols, but Mayuko would be devastated if you couldn't celebrate her special day with her.
What do you do?

Lataya and Chelsea are bright, popular, and very pretty. They are also close friends with Michelle, a shy girl who suffers from a severe case of acne. Lataya and Chelsea have been invited to the hottest party in town Saturday night, being given by two popular guys, Brandon and his brother. But the boys cruelly stated that Michelle would absolutely not be welcome at the party.
What would you do if you were in the girls' place?

When girls reach their teens, sometimes their female friends take a back seat. Suddenly, the subject of boys becomes an ever-fascinating topic of discussion. Who's cute? Who isn't? Which guy would you love to kiss? This period is a normal stage of development.

Right now, one of the biggest dilemmas you may face is making a choice between doing something with a boyfriend or having fun with your girlfriends. You may feel that you can be with the girls any old time, but a date with an exciting guy is a special occasion.

Think about how you would feel in the following situation:

You and your best friend had been planning for weeks to go to your favorite band's concert together. The two of you had spent hours discussing what you would wear, who would be there, where you would eat afterward. You had fun arguing about which song the band should use to close their show. Then, at the very last minute — actually, the very afternoon of the performance — your friend calls. "I know you'll understand," she says. "Rob called," she continues, "and he asked me out for tonight. I just couldn't say no. I've been waiting for him to show some interest in me since the day I first saw him. Why don't you ask Jen or Candy to go to the concert with you?"

Your feelings about boys shift from day to day. On Monday, you're absolutely in love with gorgeous Jason in your math class; by Wednesday, you're giving him the cold shoulder because he hasn't called you in two days. When you're thinking about the boy of your dreams, it may be hard to concentrate on anything else, like studying, doing housework, or preparing for your Girl Scout troop meeting. But what about the girl who doesn't seem to have an interest in the opposite sex? Perhaps she is shy or maybe she is not ready to think about a relationship. She may simply have other interests right now. Or maybe she's just not interested in boys in a romantic way.

Remember, right now you shouldn't be under pressure to be part of a couple. This is a great time to make friends of both sexes, hang out, prepare for your future, and start on the path that might lead to fulfillment of dreams. You have many exciting years ahead of you — there is no need to be part of a twosome to feel complete.

You know what would be enlightening and a lot of fun?
Why don't you and some of your friends get together
with your mothers, female guardians, or aunts, and talk
to them about what life was like when they were
teenagers. Ask to see photographs, theater and concert
programs, magazine clippings. Most likely, very few of
them married the guy they were dating in high school.
And it's also probable that they will urge you to live it up
and enjoy your carefree teenage years instead of getting
totally wrapped up in a love relationship.

Decisions About Relationships: The Choice Is Yours
One of the most difficult and emotional issues that comes
up related to dating concerns sexual activity. Some of the
risks to consider are:

• Feelings of guilt over going against moral or
  religious values.

• Problems with parents.

• The trauma of finding out that your partner did
  not share your expectations of future commitment.

• Unwanted pregnancy.

• Sexually transmitted diseases.

Below is a list of specific ways you can support your
decision to abstain from having sex.

• Avoid situations where you might feel pressured to
  have sex. For example, Vincent has asked you to watch
  television at his house when his parents are away, or
  Cliff asks you to drive down to the lake with him at
  midnight.

- Remember you always have the right to say no, even if you have said yes before.

- Practice saying no by role-playing with friends or by saying no in other situations.

- Avoid dating older boys or men, who generally expect more from girls and may apply more pressure.

- Go out with groups of boys and girls, or double-date.

- Don't agree to do something just because you don't want to hurt a boy's feelings. Saying no to sex doesn't have to mean rejecting him as a person.

- Be honest from the start in your dating relationships. Let your date know your real feelings about sexual activity through both your words and your actions.

Date Rape

When you're planning a romantic date with a special guy, the last thing you want to think about is the possibility that he might physically attack you. Most boys will probably listen when you say no or show no interest in sexual activity. Unfortunately, some boys may become aggressive and demanding. Today, a lot of girls have serious concerns about protecting themselves from potential physical harm on a date. The incidence of "date rape" — forced sex by a man she knows — is cause for concern. Although it can happen to anyone, the crime of rape more frequently occurs to young women.

Over 80 percent of rape victims were acquainted with their assailants; only 5 percent of these victims reported their rapes to the police.

There are ways that you can protect yourself. Here are some tips to help you stay safe:

- Don't accept a ride with a boy(s) you don't know very well.

- Avoid going alone to hangout spots where crowds of guys tend to behave aggressively.

- At a party, don't go off outside or into a secluded room with a boy who has had too much to drink. If you think a date is acting very aggressively, be firm in saying you're not interested. Move off to another group of friends.

- Call your parents or other responsible adult if you need someone to come and get you.

- Never let a boy try to intimidate you into having sex against your will. Ignore the old lines like "Prove you're a woman" and "If you loved me, you would do it." Remember the expression, "No means no."

- Let your parent/guardian know where you will be on your date.

Date rape is a subject that you may want to discuss in depth with a parent/guardian, a religious adviser, a teacher, or a Girl Scout leader.

You have probably heard the words "peer pressure" many times. Maybe your parents have cautioned you about getting involved with the wrong crowd, or your teachers have told you about the merits of being an individual and not conforming to another person's ideals. Perhaps your religious leader has talked about acting on your own principles and adhering to an internal set of values, not an externally imposed set of standards.

In principle, it is easy to understand why you should not succumb to negative peer pressure, but in many situations the old adage "It's easier said than done" applies. Frequently, it is a desire to belong and to fit in with a certain group that creates stress in the lives of teenagers. In other words, you may be in a situation where your friends are doing something that you know you really shouldn't do but you want to be a part of the crowd and you do it anyway, against your better judgment.

The resulting feelings of confusion, stress, and guilt can have an impact on your mental health. To overcome the negative consequences of peer pressure, try to avoid situations where you know you might do something you really don't want to do. Also, try to assess each decision you make and to think about the long-term consequences.

Positive mental health is an asset because it enables you to feel good about yourself and your accomplishments. When peer pressure causes you to engage in activities that are incongruous with your values and principles, you relinquish a portion of your stable mental health. Be aware of the effects of peer pressure and try to discern when it's okay to "go along with the crowd" and when you really must stand on your own and make your own decisions in order to retain your pride and psychological well-being.

Family Dynamics

Family dynamics frequently complicate the lives of teenagers. One day your parents/guardians are treating you like an adult with plenty of responsibility, and the next, they are treating you like a child who must be constantly watched and guided. Or, sometimes your brothers and sisters seem like your best friends, people with whom you can laugh hysterically, or talk seriously. And at other times, they are in your way, invading your space, using your things and intruding on your privacy.

I Am

I am unique but not always appreciated
I wonder what happens when you die
I hear whispers in the night
I see starving kids in Africa
I want to be myself
I am unique but not always appreciated

I pretend to be more than I am
I feel I can excel throughout my existence
I touch the thoughts of others
I worry about how people think about me
I cry when I think I will fail
I am unique but not always appreciated

I understand myself more than anyone
I say I will do my best to succeed
I dream that I will find myself
I try to help those in need
I hope the human situation will improve
I am unique but not always appreciated

Debbie Folz, 14
Winema Girl Scout Council,
Oregon

Maybe your family has undergone a divorce and remarriage, and you have acquired stepbrothers and stepsisters. Each of these occurrences can contribute to a host of emotions ranging from depression, anger, and guilt to confusion and insecurity.

No matter how your family is constructed, the dynamics that you experience will certainly play a major role in your mental health. If your family life gives you a sense of security, you will probably be better able to excel in your endeavors and to achieve your goals. If you are constantly fearful of hurt and rejection from family members, this may inhibit you from trying new things.

Life's Flight

Like a bird you have given
me the wings to fly,
The strength and courage
to claim the sky,
A breeze to lift me from my
own shaky wings,
Saving me from the rains
that immaturity brings.
My family has been a pond
to drink when I thirst
for love,

And when life leaves me
flying how you lift me
above.
All my problems, misfortune
and most of all the pain,
And when it was over you
were my confidence, my
reason to sing.

Dishile Davis, 15
Audubon Girl Scout Coun
Louisiana

Stress Reducers

When life feels frenzied, chaotic, and somewhat out of control, what can you do? People deal with stress in a variety of ways. The list below offers some suggestions for different activities that can help you to gain a new perspective on problems or areas of your life that are particularly troublesome.

- Take a long walk.

- Play a sport.

- Read a funny book or magazine.

- Call a friend on the telephone.

- Write a story, poem, or letter.

- Play with young children.

- Listen to your favorite tapes or CDs.

- Talk to a family member.

- Draw or paint a picture.

- Work on a new interest project.

- Garden indoors or out.

- Record your thoughts or feelings in a journal or diary.

- Play your favorite computer or video game.

- Go shopping.

- Reevaluate your clothes for new fashion ideas.

Heeding healthy living habits.

Exercising your mind and body regularly.

Appreciating yourself and your unique abilities.

Learning about contemporary health issues like AIDS.

Taking time to develop relationships with your peers.

Having fun with family and friends.

Sample Service Projects

- Provide child care at women's health clinics in your community.

- Volunteer at a suicide prevention hotline.

- Take training so you can raise a guide dog for the blind or a hearing dog for the deaf.

- Help deliver food to homebound seniors or AIDS patients by working with an existing organization.

- Be part of a traveling drama troop that highlights adolescent problems.

- Sponsor a family forum for contemporary issues, with speakers, workshops, and displays.

- Start a pet visitation program for a local retirement or nursing home.

- Sponsor a "Safe at Home Alone" workshop for younger children who are home alone. Give them safety and coping tips for dealing with strangers, siblings, and schoolwork.

- Refurbish a room at a women's shelter.

Careers in Health

Cardiologist

Supervisor of crisis hotline

Dance therapist

Dentist

Director of hospital outpatient services

Pharmacist

Director of community health nursing

Anesthesiologist

Biochemistry technologist

Licensed practical nurse

Ophthalmologist

Psychologist

Pediatrician

Paramedic

Supervisor, blood donor recruiters

Ultrasound technologist

Family therapist

CHAPTER THREE

Leadership in Action

Are you a leader? A seemingly simple question with so many complex answers. Many young women would state yes without delay, and others would answer no without hesitation. A person's response depends largely on her definition of leadership.

Perhaps you think that leadership is confined just to those people who have been elected or appointed to a position of authority, or who have an official title. Or, maybe your idea of a leader is much broader, and includes someone who has a unique way of visualizing what needs to be done or how things should be accomplished. As you begin to examine the who, what, where, when, why, and how of leadership it is almost certain that you will be able to identify situations in which you have taken the lead.

Becoming a Leader

When you think of leadership, you might not consider the unusual, groundbreaking work of individuals who simply refuse to accept the prevailing wisdom or conventional way of looking at things. But that's often the essence of leadership — vision, the ability to perceive things before others do. For example, Barbara McClintock's male colleagues dismissed her work in DNA research, but her discoveries revolutionized the field of developmental biology and ultimately earned her a Nobel Prize in medicine.

Leadership and Women

Women have often been excluded from the lists of leaders because men's accomplishments have traditionally received more acclaim. However, a great many women have made striking achievements in their fields. At right are descriptions of accomplishments made by ten outstanding women. Below is a list of the women who made these accomplishments (not given in the same order). Can you match each woman with her respective accomplishments? Write in a letter beside each woman's name.

1 Georgia O'Keeffe

2 Beatrix Jones Farrand

3 Maya Lin

4 Wilma Mankiller

5 Wilma Rudolph

6 Maria Cadilla de Martínez

7 Verina Morton Harris Jones

8 Judith E. Heuman

9 Florence Bascom

10 Nydia Velázquez

A Outstanding Olympic medalist, who overcame polio in her youth to become a record-breaking track star.

B Received first Ph.D. in geology at Johns Hopkins University; sat behind a screen in classes because of her gender.

C Principal Chief of the Cherokee Nation.

D Folklorist and writer; only woman admitted to the Puerto Rican Historical Academy in 1934.

E An Assistant Secretary in the U.S. Department of Education; successfully sued a local board of education because they did not want to hire teachers who used wheelchairs.

F Founder, along with Frederick Law Olmstead, of the American Society of Landscape Architects.

G American artist, born in 1887, who was known for her brilliant paintings of flowers and stark landscapes.

H First woman to practice medicine in Mississippi; head of Lincoln Settlement House in New York City, which housed a free kindergarten and a day nursery.

I Yale architectural student who designed the Vietnam Veterans Memorial in Washington, D.C.

J First Puerto Rican-born member of Congress, elected to the House of Representatives in 1993.

Can you identify people whom you know personally who can be called leaders? The captain of a sports team, the organizer of a substance abuse prevention program at school, the Girl Scout who often comes up with creative ways to obtain agreement about troop plans, religious leaders, and teachers are some of the individuals who might come to mind.

What Is a Leader?

Leaders come from all walks of life. They come from different professions, ethnic backgrounds, socioeconomic levels, geographic areas, and political parties. Despite all these differences, however, leaders usually perform some of the same functions. For example, they:

- Shape visions and goals.

- Help a group make decisions and reach goals.

- Resolve conflicts.

- Motivate others.

- Attract, support, and defend the work of a group.

- Collaborate with other groups.

- Delegate tasks and responsibilities.

Learning to perform these functions takes time and practice. For example, some people find it difficult to delegate responsibility because they think that if they want something done right they have to do it themselves. As you adopt more leadership roles, you will continually redefine and evaluate what tactics, techniques, and styles work best for you.

Courage

*I am courage, standing up to someone
of authority.
I come from both your mind and heart,
making your thoughts and ideas burst
out with confidence.
I am as old as life and as young as
an infant learning to walk.
My sister is bravery, we fight for what
we believe in.
I like to make you think and use your
opinions, letting your adrenaline go.
I am an exciting and loud feeling,
a voice in your mind pushing you.
I am courage.*

> Karin Brereton, 14
> Muir Trail Girl Scout Council,
> California

Finding Your Leadership Style

There are many distinct styles of leadership. Some
people lead by democracy, adhering to group decision-
making processes. Others lead by dictatorship, giving
all the orders. Different styles of leadership work well
in different settings and for different people.

For example, Girl Scouting's model of leadership is called
girl/adult partnership. This model requires adults to be
facilitators, a role in which they relinquish control and
decision-making to girls. Rather than dictating behavior
and activities, a Girl Scout leader helps girls to become
everything *they* wish to be. What are some of the attributes
of an effective Girl Scout leader? How does the role of the
Girl Scout leader compare with that of other leaders?

Here are some strategies for helping you to define your own leadership style:

1. Make a list of famous people whom you consider good leaders. Ensure that your list includes both women and men, and people from cultures that are different from your own. Go to your local library or bookstore and find books or magazine articles about them. Decide which leaders you most identify with.

2. Make a list of people you know who have leadership ability. Next to their names, write the qualities they possess that make them good leaders. Which person is most like you? Ask that person what she or he thinks makes her or him a leader.

3. In your local library, find the biographies of four famous women, some of whom are representative of your ethnic, cultural, religious, or geographical roots. In what fields did they distinguish themselves? Were they leaders? What do you have in common with them?

4. Make a list of the leadership roles you have already assumed in Girl Scouting, in school, or in your community. How did you get these positions? What gave you the most satisfaction in each situation? What was your greatest accomplishment as a leader? Have you refused or turned down a leadership position? What were your reasons? In retrospect, were you wise to refuse?

Use the following scenarios to think about and to discuss with others your own leadership style:

• You have been selected to be manager of the stage crew for the local summer stock theater. This means

that you must secure all necessary props and oversee the construction of certain parts of the scenery. You will be working with several people your own age and some who are older than you. Some individuals, however, will not take you seriously and others just want to goof around and have fun. They keep telling you to "lighten up." What do you do? How do you motivate the group? What measures do you take to ensure that the job gets done well?

- You are a lifeguard assigned to "family hour" at the county swimming pool. This facility has a number of very specific rules, including one stipulating that children under five must be supervised by an adult. For two weeks in a row, the same family has dropped its children off, the youngest of whom is only three. Each time you tell them that the child must be supervised by an adult and they tell you that their twelve-year-old daughter will be in charge. You know this is not appropriate. How do you exercise your role as the leader in charge of the pool?

- You have been elected junior class president of your high school. During your campaign you made a number of promises, including institution of a broader sports program, lunch hour off of school premises, and greater freedom during periods when students do not have classes. How will you work with other school officials to accomplish these objectives? How will you get other students involved? Whom will you select to help you with the work?

Contemplating these situations should help you to realize that being a leader is a complex task that requires creativity, hard work, and commitment. Most good leaders, moreover, have excellent interpersonal skills and are able to communicate effectively. In some cases, individuals are able to lead on the basis of charisma, or the fact that other individuals are simply drawn to them as people.

Where Do You Find Leadership Opportunities?

Opportunities to enjoy positions of leadership can be found at school, on your job, in your extracurricular activities, in your religious group, or in your community. Find a forum where you feel comfortable exerting your skills and taking on a leadership role.

Girl Scouting in particular offers numerous ways in which young women can serve as leaders. Both within the troop/group environment and at the council level, girls have a wide array of formal and informal opportunities to take the lead on projects and committees. Not only can you earn the Senior Girl Scout Leadership Award, but you can become a member of a council planning or advisory board, or other group concerned with developing councilwide activities.

Other leadership opportunities specifically for Senior Girl Scouts are as follows:

Senior Girl Scout Program Aide

As a Senior Girl Scout Program Aide, you work directly with a troop or camp unit of younger girls under the supervision of an adult volunteer or staff member. You are required to participate in approximately 10 hours of training, followed by 25 hours of service. Being a Program

Aide is an opportunity to share your expertise with other Girl Scouts on a variety of projects and issues. For more information, see page 150.

Leader-in-Training (LIT)

A Leader-in-Training completes a group leadership course and works with a mentor leader in a Daisy, Brownie, Junior, or Cadette Girl Scout troop. A Leader-in-Training project usually spans a five- to eight-month period, with the time divided between course sessions and 25 hours of actual work with a troop or other Girl Scout group. A Leader-in-Training must have completed ninth grade before beginning this project.

Senior Girl Scout Troop Assistant

A Senior Girl Scout who wants to assist a Girl Scout leader with an established troop can become a troop assistant. To take on this role, you must have completed your LIT project, have completed the tenth grade, and be able to make a full-year commitment to a troop.

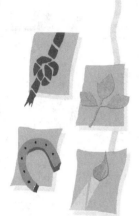

Counselor-in-Training (CIT)

A Counselor-in-Training project offers older Girl Scouts the opportunity to work with children in the out-of-doors. A Counselor-in-Training completes an outdoor group leadership course before interning as a counselor in a Girl Scout camp. The training includes regular hours devoted to classes, plus actual experience in camp units where the CIT works directly with the girls under the supervision of a camp counselor or unit leader. This opportunity is available to Senior Girl Scouts who have completed the tenth grade.

In your second year of training, when you become a **Counselor-in-Training II**, you will have opportunities to concentrate in a particular area. You might become a high adventure specialist, a horse instructor, a nature specialist, an art specialist, or even work in the areas of administration or maintenance of a camp. Your council should have further information about this opportunity.

Apprentice Trainers

Senior Girl Scouts who have completed an LIT project may gain further leadership experience by becoming Apprentice Trainers. As an Apprentice Trainer, you will receive training that will enable you to teach others about a special area.

Young Adult Members of a Standing Committee of the National Board

A very small number of Senior Girl Scouts are selected every three years to serve as members of standing committees of the National Board of Directors of Girl Scouts of the U.S.A. Although they cannot vote, these young women have the opportunity to express their opinions and to do other work requested of Board members. For example, the girls who serve on the Membership and Program Committee review drafts of the girls' handbooks and suggest revisions.

Ask the leader of your troop or group for more details about any of these leadership opportunities. In addition, GSUSA provides your council with a publication outlining the details of each of these projects.

When Should You Try to Be a Leader?

On many occasions you may want to take the lead in accomplishing a goal, finishing a project, or facilitating the work of a group. In other situations, however, you may wish to defer the major leadership responsibilities to someone else. Perhaps you do not feel that you have the specific skills or the time required to do a good job. Maybe you are trying to join a new group and you want to find out more about the way it works. Perhaps you simply prefer to have less responsibility than would be required of a leader. All these are valid reasons for opting for a less visible, non-leadership position. And, remember that as a team member, you still get to express your opinions, accomplish tasks, develop communication skills, and influence others.

Why Become a Leader?

Adopting a position of authority and responsibility can have many positive consequences. As a leader of a group or project, you can hone the skills necessary to get the job done, improve your confidence, and enhance your ability to deal with other people. Leading a group is also a way to show other people that you care enough to work with them on their behalf. You will derive a great sense of satisfaction and achievement when things turn out as you planned.

Taking on leadership roles will also prepare you for work and for good citizenship. In every profession or trade, employers value initiative and the ability to get the job done. Both of these qualities are associated with leaders, and you can become quite adept at them through practice. In addition, you can highlight your leadership experiences in job interviews or in applications for college or vocational school.

How Can You Become a Leader?

Many times people choose not to accept the role of leader because they are afraid of failing. Often, however, they do have the necessary skills, and it is simply a matter of overcoming inhibitions and taking risks. For example, some people do not think of themselves as leaders because they have not led a group in a traditional way. However, the qualities of thinking critically and acting independently are also signs of leadership. As you become more comfortable with the knowledge that you can make decisions for yourself, you will more easily assume leadership roles in a group.

Here are some ways you can learn more about leadership in general:

1. Ask your Girl Scout council about leadership opportunities sponsored by GSUSA or by the council.

2. Check with local community centers to find out if they have leadership programs for young people.

3. Read books and magazine articles on leadership and female leaders.

4. Ask your teachers about leaders of diverse backgrounds and leaders with disabilities.

5. Seek out women in your community who are in leadership roles in health care, government, education, the arts, and business. Ask them if you can speak with them, or invite them as guests to speak to your troop/group on the subject of leadership.

6. Think about your own spiritual discipline or religious tradition. How does it empower you, give you courage, motivate you to serve, clarify your goals and vision? Does it also provide an encouraging community? Can it help you to try again if you fail? Does it help you to put things in perspective?

Footprints in Time

I always remember —
and am reminded
    of people.
Just ordinary people,
all who did something extraordinary.
They all left behind one thing —

    Footprints in Time

And on that long stretch of sidewalk,
As we walk along —
We try to fit our footprints into those
of others.

In reality though,
We'll never fill their shoes.
We should just keep walking,
Hold our heads up straight —
    And wait.
Wait until our feet sink in —
and we are able to make our
own footprints.

Our own Footprints in Time

    Dana Latimer, 17
    Conifer Girl Scout Council,
    Arkansas

Group Dynamics

Membership in groups and organizations is an integral part of life. You are already a member of many groups — cultural, racial, religious, and family groups. In general, people organize around a common set of values, principles, and goals. Some organizations are very formally structured, with elected officials, written rules, and specific criteria for membership. Other groups are much more informally arranged, with shared leadership, changing membership, and flexible standards for admission.

Functioning as a member of a group is a skill that everyone must learn. In any organization, you may at some time experience frustration because you believe there is inadequate leadership, a lack of commitment from other members, inefficient systems for accomplishing the work, or not enough human or financial resources. Whatever the deficiencies, however, you can learn to improve the problem situations while you accomplish your goals.

Take a moment to analyze a group that you are very familiar with. Is this group formally or informally organized? Is it systematic and efficient? Does it accomplish its articulated goals? What style of leadership is present? If you could, how would you change the group dynamics?

As a Girl Scout you have many opportunities to develop your skills at working in a group. Many girls belong to troops or groups where they must constantly discuss, negotiate, compromise, and cooperate in order to accomplish the group's objectives as well as the goals of individual members.

Each time you embark on another project with your Girl Scout troop, the dynamics of the group might change. For example, the girl who took the lead in organizing a career seminar might take a secondary role in arranging a community sports tournament. In other words, the manner in which leadership positions are assumed will depend upon the types of tasks involved. When a project arises for which you have a particular expertise or interest, you can volunteer to take the lead. Sometimes, people around you who see your abilities will provide the encouragement and the incentive to enable you to accept the leadership role.

Conflict Resolution

General Rules from the Experts

Conflict is a part of life that people generally like to avoid. While conflict is stressful, it can also serve as a learning and growing experience.

Sometimes you have disagreements with your friends and with members of your family. In school, you may be called upon to defend an unpopular cause, or feel compelled to speak on behalf of someone who is not being treated fairly. In all these circumstances, you will be involved in a conflict.

Experts who write about conflict resolution all mention some basic strategies. First, separate the cause of the conflict from the person or group of people you are having the conflict with. That's not easy to do, especially if you are having a disagreement with your best friend or with members of your family.

Suppose you and your best friend are on your way to take a math test. She asks you to let her copy from your paper during the exam. You're very good at math, and she's missed some classes and is afraid she'll fail. She would have asked you to help her study, but she didn't want to bother you this weekend. What would you do? How can you separate the person from the cause of the conflict in this situation?

You believe that cheating is wrong, and that your friend should never ask you to do such a thing. On the other hand, you don't want to make her angry by preaching to her about the evils of cheating. After all, she's probably heard it all before. But you can't bring yourself to give in.

When confronted with this kind of conflict, experts suggest that one strategy is to talk about solutions. You can suggest that your friend ask the teacher to give her the test a few days later, especially since she missed several classes. Then you can offer to help her study during that time. You can also ask your friend to suggest some solutions, saying that you would rather not engage in what you consider cheating.

People disagree with each other because they value different things. What you value is based on how you were brought up and on your cultural background, race, socioeconomic group, religious beliefs, and view of the world. For instance, in some Asian cultures, group consensus is the model for solving problems in the workplace — everyone in the group must agree before moving forward. This is different from the way that Americans generally view conflict resolution at work. Americans go by the "majority rule" theory, in which the minority submits to the will of the majority. In both cases, some negotiation will take place, and people are likely to bargain with one another, but there's a very fundamental difference in approach and in values.

Commitment

Dreams become reality,
Goals are achieved,
Challenges are overcome,
Tasks are completed, and
Friendships remain strong
because of:
    COMMITMENT
The bond that cements
the details in place,
Fueled by the determination
to accomplish the best.
A surge of energy that takes the lead,
Giving heart and soul to make it happen.
Focus on reaching and grasping the product:
    COMMITMENT.

Bea Barber, 17
Goldenrod Girl Scout Council,
Nebraska

In the example of two friends who must resolve a conflict over cheating, what does each young woman value? Suppose that your friend feels that asking for the answers to the test is not cheating. She thinks that it's okay to do that for a friend, that she would do it if she were in your place. You point out that you think it's cheating, and that you would never ask a friend to do that for you. You and your friend do not share the same values in this case.

Generally, in interpersonal relationships, men tend to be competitive and prone to conflict whereas women tend to be cooperative.

Instead of arguing, it might be more helpful to ask your friend, "Since I can't do what you ask, what *can* I do to help you?" In other words, talk about the different ways you can resolve this conflict. You may realize that you don't want to be friends, or that you want to remain friends but that around some issues you'll have to negotiate a solution. Talk about the resolution: Will it be a resolution that preserves your friendship? Should that resolution be a "rule" of your friendship or just a temporary measure? Discussing things in this way may get to the real issues.

It is important when trying to resolve a conflict that everyone involved take the time to understand each other, and that the individuals or the group allow enough time to reach a reasonable solution. Some conflicts will end with people "agreeing to disagree," or with a temporary truce, just as nations call a truce in the midst of a war in order to reflect on the conflict.

"Good Conflict"

You probably find yourself choosing friends who share your values, but as you already know, you are often in the position of working with someone who has values very different from your own. The conflicts that arise may be an opportunity to learn something about another person as well as about yourself.

Conflict makes people aware of things that they have not yet resolved for themselves. Suppose you go to the movies with a friend and the film turns out to be a comedy which pokes fun at women who are so worried about gaining weight that they will do anything, including starving themselves, to remain thin. You think the film is terrible, and your friend thinks you're overreacting. After discussing it, you realize that *you're* afraid of getting fat, and you resented the fact that the filmmaker made fun of that fear.

Some conflicts are real learning experiences. Suppose you work at a local fast food restaurant on Saturdays and Sundays. You notice that a co-worker rushes out every Saturday at least 15 minutes before the shift ends. One day, she fails to clean a table and you have to clear it. You tell her the next day that you're getting a little tired of her behavior, and you think it's unfair that she leaves early. She apologizes and says, "I have to attend religious services on Saturday at 5:00, and if I don't leave at a quarter of, I don't get there on time." You're surprised because everyone you know attends religious services on Sundays. You ask her about this, and she begins to tell you about her religion. You realize that you've learned something. Where you thought there was going to be a conflict, there was actually an opportunity to help someone, and in the bargain learn about a person who is different from you.

Gender Differences

When people are able to recognize and celebrate the ways in which they are different, they can reduce conflict and create an atmosphere in which they all feel comfortable expressing themselves. That does not mean there will be no conflict — it just means that the conflicts will probably be resolved in a way that doesn't hurt people.

Do men and women really think differently? It's hard to make judgments about men and women without creating stereotypes, but sometimes it seems that women and men really do value different things, communicate differently, and approach life with different standards. Some experts think that women tend to value cooperation when they're speaking to others and that men tend to be more competitive. These differing styles could lead to conflict in some situations.

While people should never make assumptions about others according to their gender or their culture or any of the other ways in which people are different, remember to take these characteristics into consideration in any conflict.

Groups have all kinds of conflicts, and many of them are struggles for power or control. Conflict resolution may take longer in a group because many more personalities are involved. But experts have noted that a group conflict can be resolved through some of the same steps one would use in resolving a conflict between two people.

1. Identify the conflict. What is the underlying value that is creating the conflict?

2. Discuss how each member of the group thinks about the conflict, and how she or he views its importance.

3. Discuss potential solutions and the methods that could be used to reach those solutions.

4. Designate someone to facilitate the resolution who is not involved in the conflict. Have that person ask the group to identify any similarities in the solutions they've suggested.

5. After the group comes to some kind of resolution, try to create guidelines for dealing with any future conflicts of this kind.

Public Speaking

At one time or another, almost everyone is requested to give a talk in front of a group. Many people fear speaking in public, and it is only through much practice and effort that these apprehensions are overcome.

Some common tips can make public speaking easier. Be prepared. Know your material, but do not try to memorize an answer or a speech. Instead, develop a clear idea about the facts that you want to present and state them in a manner that "flows" rather than in a precise "memorized" format. Use notes if they help you feel comfortable, but try to look at the group most of the time. It is sometimes helpful to start your presentation by concentrating your gaze on one individual who appears friendly. If looking directly at people makes you uncomfortable, direct your gaze just above everyone's head.

Many shy teenagers grow up to be renowned public speakers.

Colorful examples and touches of humor will liven up your presentation. As with many other skills, "practice makes perfect," so you should begin by volunteering to speak in situations where you feel comfortable — for instance, at your Girl Scout meetings or at Girl Scout council events. Remember that you're probably your own harshest critic. The people listening to you probably won't hear the tremor in your voice or notice your knees shaking. And those signs of anxiety will lessen as your talk continues.

Parliamentary Procedure

Parliamentary procedure is a method of discussion and decision-making that is particularly useful when large groups of people meet. This procedure is often used at board, school, and government meetings. The procedure is also employed in the meetings of the Girl Scout National Council.

Parliamentary procedure is a democratic system by which all members of a group are able to express their opinions on an issue or question. Decisions are made by voting or by some form of general agreement. To learn more about this method, attend meetings in your community where parliamentary procedure is used or read about it. One well-known book is *Robert's Rules of Order* by Henry M. Robert. You might also refer to *Parliamentary Procedures at a Glance* by O. Garfield Jones and *Pointers on Parliamentary Procedure* from the National Association of Parliamentarians.

Below are some of the more common terms used in parliamentary procedure.

Term	Meaning
Adjourn	To end a meeting
Agenda	A list of items in the order that they will be brought up at the meeting
Amendment	A change made to a motion
Division	A call for a standing vote
Majority	More than half of the voters
Minutes	An accurate record of the group's actions and decisions
Motion	A brief statement of a proposed action
Point of information	A request for information or clarification
Point of order	An objection made because of a perceived improper procedure
Quorum	The number of voting participants needed to transact business — usually a majority of the group
Second	A second person who supports a motion; required before discussion or voting
Standing vote	A vote in which the participants show their position on a question by standing up or raising their hands

Once you have learned about parliamentary procedure, practice using it as a group at some of your Girl Scout meetings.

Developing an Agenda

An agenda, an orderly list of things to be done, can help a meeting run smoothly. Keep these ideas in mind:

- Decide on the order of items, keeping related ones together.

- Set approximate time limits for each topic.

- Share the proposed agenda with members and get their input.

Be sure to follow the agenda at the meeting. Toward the end of the meeting, ask for agenda items for the next meeting.

Minutes

It's a good idea to have one member responsible for taking notes, or minutes, during or shortly after a meeting. Minutes can serve as a record of decisions reached, areas of disagreement, and future plans. Remember to note:

- Decisions and general agreements.

- The number of votes for and against a motion (especially important if your group's votes will be added to others for the final outcome).

- How jobs were divided, who was responsible for what, and any suggestions for improvement.

Reporting back, updating members who were absent, and building the next agenda all are made easier by complete and accurate note-taking.

Listening to the viewpoints and opinions of others.

Empowering people to "be their best."

Achieving consensus through lively debate.

Delegating tasks and facilitating work.

Employing the unique skills of each member of the group.

Reacting constructively to adversity.

Stretching imaginations and bolstering self-esteem.

Helping others to accomplish goals.

Initiating change through vision and hard work.

Practicing fair and ethical decision-making policies.

Sample Service Projects

- Develop kits containing materials that can help girls complete Brownie Girl Scout Try-Its and badge activities. Work with your council to publicize the existence of these kits, which might be used at camps and other properties.

- Act as a resource in assisting a first-year leader and her troop to plan and go on a camping trip.

- Become an officer at school or in a youth group of your religious organization.

- Show the need for a stop sign or stoplight in an unsafe intersection for pedestrians, and convince your community government to install one.

- Take a Red Cross first-aid course and then volunteer your skills in the community.

- Form a corps of young people who can respond to help in emergencies, such as providing child care at shelters or emergency care for abandoned pets.

- Organize teens to respond to a world crisis affecting children, such as helping to make CARE packages, assisting with mailings, or working in community drives.

- Coach a younger girls' sports team.

- Start an environmental service club at your high school. Arrange for speakers and develop a list of service projects that the club can work on.

- Organize and maintain an ongoing "lost person's booth" at an annual community event, county fair, or street fair in cooperation with the event managers.

Leadership Careers in Government and Politics

Lawyer

Mayor

Superintendent of schools

Commissioner of public works

Director, council on aging

Judge

City manager

Foreign service officer

Department director in government funding agency

Park ranger

Police chief

Food and drug inspector

Director, arts and humanities council

Congressional district aide

State senator

Lobbyist

CHAPTER FOUR

High School and Beyond

The screen goes blank and suddenly a public
service announcement flashes across the bot-
tom of your television set . . . A cure for AIDS
has been discovered! Your heart leaps with
excitement and your imagination transports you into a
hospital lab, only this time it's you in the white coat sur-
rounded by countless test tubes, microscopes, and vials of
chemicals. . . . You've always wanted to be a doctor.

Everyone has dreams about what she or he will be in the
future. Some people derive their career aspirations from
a desire to be "rich and famous"; others strive to follow
in the footsteps of an individual whom they respect or
admire; and still more elect to carve careers out of their
skills, interests, and hobbies. Whatever the motivation,
most careers require a certain amount of preparation
through education, training, and practical experience.

Making Career Choices in High School

Establishing a career is like winding your way along a path on which each intersection leads to more choices that result in different consequences and, ultimately, more decisions. For most people, this journey is an interesting one filled with challenges, rewards, and sometimes with disappointments.

You might say, "I'm still in high school. What does all this have to do with me?" Creating a hypothetical "road map" will help to answer that question.

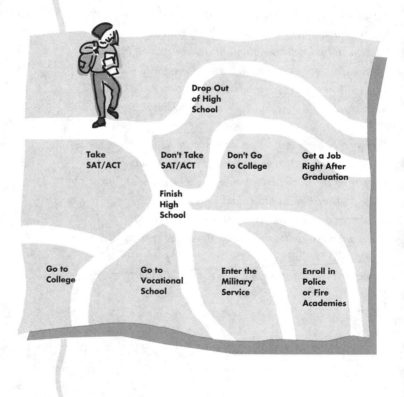

Drop Out of High School

Take SAT/ACT

Don't Take SAT/ACT

Don't Go to College

Get a Job Right After Graduation

Finish High School

Go to College

Go to Vocational School

Enter the Military Service

Enroll in Police or Fire Academies

The picture illustrates that you, as a high school student, do have a number of critical choices to make that will impact on your future. Analyzing some of these components a little more closely will be helpful.

Taking the Scholastic Assessment Test (SAT) or American College Test (ACT)

Many high school students take the Scholastic Assessment Test. This exam is composed of six parts, each of which contains questions about concepts in either math or English. The best score that you can receive on either the math or the English section is an 800, and scores can range anywhere from 200 points to 800.

The American College Test (ACT) is another standardized exam used for college admissions. The ACT is made up of four sections: English, math, reading, and science. Each of these parts is scored separately and an individual can receive between 1 point, which is the lowest possible score, and 36, which is the highest possible score. You will also receive a composite score, which is an average of the number of points that you got on the four sections.

To review for these tests, many students use special guides that are available in bookstores and public libraries. Also, some people choose to attend special SAT/ACT preparation courses offered by private companies or through high school guidance departments. Although it is generally a good idea to brush up on

In 1993, a total of 2,338,000 16-24-year-old students graduated from high school. Of these students, 1,464,000 enrolled in college.

specific concepts and to practice sample tests, the questions on the Scholastic Assessment Test and the American College Test can, for the most part, be answered from knowledge that you have been acquiring throughout your years in school.

Students who choose to attend four-year colleges are usually required to submit their scores from the SAT and/or ACT as a part of their applications. Because there is such wide variation in grading practices and curriculum content in high schools across the country, college admissions committees often use the results from the Scholastic Assessment Test or the American College Test as a standard means of comparing applications. However, colleges also consider an applicant's activities, interests, and motivation when making decisions.

Applying to College

Taking the Scholastic Assessment Test (SAT) or the American College Test (ACT), researching schools, writing essays, and going on interviews are all a part of applying to college, a complex task that requires diligence and hard work. The rewards from this effort, however, can be incredibly beneficial. Earning a college degree can open doors to many future occupations.

Helpful Hints
- Research schools carefully to determine which ones offer the types of courses and the environment that are most attractive to you. Many resources are available

for this purpose. For example, a number of companies publish books that describe details about colleges all over the country. Once you have made a preliminary list of schools that seem appealing, you should write or call each admissions office and ask for an application and a catalog. Furthermore, many video stores now have promotional tapes about different colleges.

- Be creative in your essays and thorough on your applications. Remember, the admissions committees don't know what a great person you are, so you must use your application as a vehicle for them to "get to know you." It is also helpful to ask teachers, friends, and family members to critique and proofread the written portion of your application because they may be able to remind you of important events, activities, and accomplishments that you have completely overlooked.

- Don't allow anyone to discourage you from pursuing a dream. If you really want to attend a particular school, apply even if getting in is considered a long shot. Try, however, to choose several schools — some of which you are well assured of being accepted to and some of which have more rigorous admissions standards. Also, do not let the cost of attending college prevent you from applying. Many students receive some type of financial aid either directly from a college, from a scholarship, or through a low-interest bank loan.

The first female college students were offered less rigorous courses than men, and some were required to wait on male students and wash their clothes.

Choosing a Vocational School

High school students who are interested in learning a particular trade may decide to attend vocational schools. These schools represent an opportunity to advance educationally beyond high school but do not usually demand the time and financial commitment of a four-year college. They teach students marketable skills for such careers as acting, drafting, computer programming, plumbing, word processing, retailing, and printing as well as a wide range of other specialties. If a vocational school will enable you to achieve your goals, research the possibilities carefully and select the school that offers the best program and job placement record.

Together with your friends, it may be fun to create a "map" that more thoroughly details some of the decisions that you will be making about your future. Perhaps one person could start and then everyone else could add another path or decision to the picture.

Your map might include decisions such as:

- College or vocational school.

- Summer job or recreational activities.

- Part-time job or extracurricular activities.

- Travel.

The World of Work

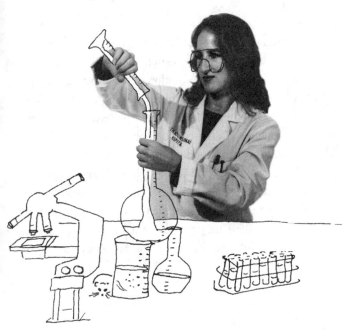

How Do People Choose an Occupation?

Throughout the course of their work lives, most people
have more than one job. In fact, research shows that people often change jobs six, seven, or more times. Factors
that contribute to the positions that you choose include:
the type of work, the level of responsibility, the nature of
the organization, the setting, and the qualifications necessary to perform successfully in a particular position.
Experts in the field of career development have designed
a variety of standardized tests that help to determine
which types of professions are best suited to different
individuals. You may want to consult your guidance
counselor or the local librarian about when and where
these tests might be given.

You can also personally assess what you like and dislike and consider how these preferences translate into components of a job. For example: Do you like to work with people or tools or ideas? If you answered people, perhaps you would like to be a doctor or a social worker or a college professor. Do you like to solve problems, or do you prefer to be given explicit instructions about how a task should be done? Someone who likes to solve problems might enjoy becoming an engineer, a labor relations mediator, or a systems analyst. Do you like to work indoors or outdoors? Someone who chooses indoors probably will not become a forest ranger or a member of the coast guard. Do you prefer to work alone or in a team? If you like to work independently, you probably would not choose to become a member of a dance troupe or theater group. Contemplating these types of questions can help you to evaluate which aspects of a job you truly value and which ones you would be willing to compromise on.

Either alone or together with your friends, brainstorm additional questions that will help you understand your preferences and values in terms of a job. Issues you might want to consider are: balancing work and other responsibilities (such as family); interests and hobbies; the atmospheres of various organizations; salary ranges; and the social implications involved in working in different companies or organizations. For example, some people might not feel comfortable working in the tobacco or alcohol industries, while others may not like to work for political organizations. A job that demands a fair amount of travel may or may not be appealing. You might want to use the *Occupation Outlook Handbook* in order to see how these variables relate to specific jobs. Even though your views on these issues will probably change throughout your career, it is fun and interesting to consider how you and your peers feel about them today.

Important Stages of Job Hunting

Preparing a Résumé

Getting a job generally begins with a résumé. A résumé can be compared to an artist's self-portrait except that it uses words instead of images. It is important for your résumé to convey an accurate, yet glowing, picture of your accomplishments and abilities, as well as the way in which these factors will benefit prospective employers. A résumé can be constructed in a variety of ways, and each individual must choose the style that is best suited to her needs. The sample résumé shown on the next page has been written in an adapted chronological format. The résumé outlines the objectives, skills, work experience, hobbies, and interests of "Sara Jones." Note that the descriptions are filled with precise, action words that convey a message about what "Sara" actually did or does.

Sara Jones
810 Tulip Way
Garden City, Nebraska 86742
(402) 000-0000
Internet: Sara@server.neb

Objective: To obtain a position for the summer that will enable me to utilize my scientific research skills to their fullest potential.

Education: Central High School, graduating in 1997.

Skills: Knowledgeable about research methods; strong writing, organizational, and inter-personal skills.

Experience:

Intern, Botanical Gardens, Omaha, Nebraska
Delivered workshops to children. Propagated plants. Oversaw feeding and fertilization of plants in the greenhouse.
  Summer 1994

Tour Guide, Nebraska State Science Museum, Omaha, Nebraska
Prepared activities and exhibits. Explained exhibits to groups. Participated in the Girl Scout camp-in program.
  1993–1994

Baby-Sitter, Garden City, Nebraska
Prepare meals, ensure safety, and entertain children at the homes of three different families.
  1993–Present

Interests and Hobbies: Girl Scouting, writing, skiing, foreign languages, wind surfing.

Awards: Girl Scout Gold Award, Mayor's Service Award

Write your own résumé. Start by listing all of your jobs, including both paid and volunteer positions. You might want to include some of the activities that you do as a Girl Scout in the experience section. Next, brainstorm as many action words as possible. Now use these words to describe the responsibilities associated with each of your jobs. Many books have been written about preparing résumés, and your local librarian will be able to assist you in finding them.

The Interview

Once you have submitted your résumé to an organization, you may be invited in for an interview. Perhaps you have experienced interviewing for other purposes, like attending a wider opportunity with nationwide participation, applying to school, or becoming a member on a committee. For the most part, a job interview is a formal conversation that allows the applicant to expand upon those experiences and skills that she has described on her résumé.

For most people, interviewing is somewhat stressful. Usually this stems from a fear that they will be asked questions that they cannot answer. To avoid some of this tension, it is helpful to do a little research about the company, to thoroughly familiarize yourself with your résumé, and to believe that you are skilled and qualified for the position that you desire. You should also be aware that it is illegal for employers to ask questions regarding race, religion, color, sex, age, national origin, citizenship, disability, or marital status.

When preparing for an interview, make sure that you have an appropriate outfit to wear. Generally, conservative attire is the best choice unless there are special circumstances that warrant wearing more casual clothing.

After completing an interview, you should send the prospective employer a follow-up note. This letter serves to reinforce your talents and skills, and it also thanks the employer for taking the time to meet with you.

It might be helpful to practice interviewing with the other girls in your troop or group or with other friends. Take turns being the employer and the interviewee. Some frequently asked questions are:

• Why do you want this type of job?

• What strengths and weaknesses will you bring to this position?

- What do you see yourself doing in five years?

- Why do you want to work for this organization?

If you have the equipment, you might want to video- or audiotape these mock interviews so that you can analyze your body language and speaking voice. Make adaptations if you feel they are necessary.

The situations below can be used for your mock interviews. You and your friends may also want to create other settings that are relevant for your experiences. You might obtain the annual reports from different companies and organizations. Use these to construct hypothetical job openings and interview questions.

- You are applying to baby-sit for your mother's friend, who has an infant daughter and a six-year-old son.

- You are being interviewed for an internship at the bank.

- You are being interviewed as a candidate for a wider opportunity with nationwide participation.

The Job Application
Either before or after an interview you may be asked to complete a job application. Depending on the type of position that you are seeking, this form will ask for the same type of information that is contained on your résumé. Complete the application neatly and thoroughly, and always provide accurate information because employers can and do verify facts.

Dreams of all sizes,
Dreams go anywhere
But when we wake up
Our dreams become air.

I was in a land of giants
Of creatures great and small
But then I woke up,
What happened to them all?

I fell asleep once more,
Floating in the sky
But then I realized
I do not know how to fly.

I had one special dream that night
I had a family of my own
I had to wash and clean
I had to take care of my home.

I remembered all my younger years
Of when I was but nine
How I dreamed of being a teacher
I dreamed that all the time.

Soon I turned 11
I wanted to work in a zoo
To feed all the animals
While learning something new.

Later I turned 13
I wanted to work with kids
Feed them their lunches,
Then remove their bibs.

But sadly, the clock woke me up
I was just the same old me
But all of that taught me something
It is just fine for me to dream.

Sarah Sellers, 13
Tanasi Girl Scout Council,
Tennessee

Other Roads to the Workplace

While careers and full-time employment might seem a lifetime away, part-time and summer jobs, internships, and mentoring are very much a reality for many young women. Each of these "roads to the workplace" offers teenagers exposure to different careers as well as to a more thorough understanding of what a typical workday might entail.

Obtaining a summer or part-time job has many benefits besides simply being a source of income. For example, working in different settings will enable you to begin to evaluate what type of work you like to do, what type of atmosphere empowers you to be your most productive, and what type of manager facilitates your work. Part-time and summer employment can also help you learn what jobs or fields you definitely do not want to pursue as a future career.

Getting a summer job may be quite competitive because many high school and college students are applying for a select number of openings. Begin seeking employment early, and do not limit your search to just one organization or location. The broader your efforts are, the more likely you are to get a position that you will like.

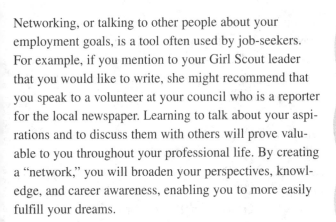

Networking, or talking to other people about your employment goals, is a tool often used by job-seekers. For example, if you mention to your Girl Scout leader that you would like to write, she might recommend that you speak to a volunteer at your council who is a reporter for the local newspaper. Learning to talk about your aspirations and to discuss them with others will prove valuable to you throughout your professional life. By creating a "network," you will broaden your perspectives, knowledge, and career awareness, enabling you to more easily fulfill your dreams.

Another option for young women is to obtain an internship. Interns generally gain exposure to many details of a specific profession. They get a chance to see, from the inside, how a business truly operates. Internships can be especially beneficial for you because they can add another credential to your résumé; they can help you to make professional contacts in a field that you might like to pursue; and they can help you to develop a sense of professionalism and pride in your business-related accomplishments.

Frequently, obtaining an internship requires some effort on your part. You must go to a library and research those companies or organizations that have internship programs. Sometimes you must complete an official application; other times, you can simply submit your résumé and a letter explaining why you would like to become an intern. With a thoughtful, well-written letter, you may even inspire an organization that had never thought about using interns to hire you.

If you have a disability that affects your writing skills, have a friend or family member help you develop a video- or audiotape that explains your motivation and skills. Don't let requirements for written material hinder you from attaining your career aspirations.

Be aware that there are many adults in the workforce who would be happy to discuss careers with you. They can talk to you about decisions they have made, and they can help guide you concerning the choices that you must make. When an adult in the workforce counsels you about your career choices on a regular basis, this individual has become your mentor. Working with an older individual in your field of interest can help you to sort out your thoughts about your future and to make decisions that will enable you to accomplish your goals.

Working with a mentor can help you to sort out your thoughts about your future and to accomplish your goals.

Women in "Real Life"

Do you sometimes dream of what your life will be like 10, 15, or 20 years from now? As teenagers, many girls have an ideal and romantic vision of "how life will be." For some young women this portrait is a very traditional one of a husband, wife, and two angelic children living in a nice home and not having any financial stresses or strain. Other girls may picture that they are high-powered, high-profile business executives in fast-paced corporations. And, many may think in terms of a combination of both. None of these pictures is good or bad, right or wrong.

For many women in today's society, working is a financial necessity. Research reveals that about 45 percent of the total workforce is female. Because so many women work outside of the home — many out of necessity, not choice — it is important for you to make decisions that will enable you to have a fulfilling, challenging career. Besides, achieving financial and professional self-sufficiency can contribute to enhanced self-esteem, which, in turn, can positively affect other areas of your life.

Despite the large number of working women, gender issues still abound in the workplace. For example, many women must contend with some form of sexual harassment at some point during their careers. Whether it is a subtle sexist joke, an openly crude remark, or some kind of inappropriate physical contact, women should not have to tolerate any sort of bias or teasing because of their gender.

If you are being sexually harassed by an employer, or anyone else for that matter, bring it to the attention of other trusted peers or adults. You should be quite vocal about how uncomfortable the comments or physical contact makes you feel. If the problems persist in the workplace, document them in writing and discuss them with your direct supervisor or the person who hired you.

Balancing Work with Other Parts of Your Life

Imagine you are 30-something. You are married and have a six-month-old child. Now you need to return to full-time work. You find a great job in your field with hours from 9:00 to 5:00, five days a week, paying $35,000 a year. You must combine your roles as homemaker and parent with your full-time paying job. Your husband must share the household chores equitably with you.

With a friend or in a small group, determine the daily household chores and activities that must be done by you and your husband on a typical working day. Your list should include at least the following items:

- Each must shower and dress.
- The dog must be walked three times a day.
- The baby must be fed breakfast.
- The baby must be dressed and brought to the baby-sitter's house.

- Each must travel to and from work.
- There must be clean laundry, especially baby clothes, for the next day.
- The baby must be picked up at the baby-sitter's.
- Dinner must be prepared and served.
- The baby must be fed dinner.
- The kitchen must be cleaned.
- The baby must be bathed and put to sleep.
- The home must be straightened up.

Decide who will do each chore, and how long each chore will take. (Don't forget to allow time for sleeping and time spent on the job.) Have each person record the information on a chart.

Tally the hours on each person's chart and record the totals. In a 24-hour workday, how much time remains for this working couple? Does one person have more time than the other? Is the work evenly divided? How much time is there for the child (playing and teaching new skills)? How much time is there to do things as a couple? How much time is there to do things alone?

Ask a group of males in your age range to do this exercise. How do your results compare with theirs?

Have your group role-play what certain times of the day (such as 6:00–8:00 in the morning, or 5:00–7:00 in the evening) might be like for the working couple.

The Future

Many changes in life can affect your career plans. Think about what you would do in each of the situations on the next page. Ask your friends for their ideas.

- The young man you are engaged to is suddenly transferred to another state and asks you to leave the college you are attending.

- You have used up all the money for education you had, and are still undecided about your future career.

- You are pregnant but want to continue to work after your child is born.

- You have been offered a promotion, but it means moving to another state. Your husband enjoys his present job and is in a field where there are few openings.

- You have talent, training, and experience, but now can't find a job in your career field.

- You have worked for many years as a volunteer, but now you need to earn money.

- You inherit a family business, but you want to become a musician.

A Final Word

Women in American society are taking more responsibility for themselves emotionally, intellectually, and economically. You can get off to a good career start by developing all of your interests and abilities while you are young. Become more knowledgeable by reading extensively. Learn more about science and technology so that you become comfortable with these subjects. The world of tomorrow is going to be a better place, and women will play a significant part in making it better!

Consider what tasks or activities you most enjoy doing.

Assess what types of jobs would maximize your skills and talents.

Research the kind of education or training necessary for the career you have chosen.

Engage in conversations with people you know who have careers that seem really exciting to you.

Enjoy your dreams, and follow them! It is you, not someone else, who can determine your future.

Remember to persevere—if you don't succeed the first time, try a second, third, fourth . . . until you get what you want.

Strive to "be your best" in all of your endeavors.

Sample Service Projects

- Help plan and present a career fair, making special efforts to invite those involved in alternative education, such as home schooling.

- Intern in a position similar to one that you would like to have in the future.

- In your local school or community center, create a resource library of educational opportunities beyond high school.

- Organize a clearinghouse for different job-shadowing experiences for girls in conjunction with "Take Your Daughter to Work Day."

- Organize study groups for students preparing to take the SAT, ACT, or other standardized tests.

- Put together a workshop on sexual harassment for girls, using resources found in your community.

- Start a baby-sitting service to help teen mothers stay in school.

Careers of the Future

Genetic counselor

Biotechnology specialist

Recycling engineer

Scientific illustrator

Computer analyst

Ethicist

Futurist

Computer-aided design (CAD) engineer

Environmental lawyer

Fiber optics engineer

Hazardous waste research specialist

Gerontologist

Research chemist

Computer journalist

Computer programmer

CHAPTER FIVE

Skills for Living—
The Amazing Balancing Act

*Things to do, people to see, places to go —
how can you fit it all in? Sometimes it may seem
that there are not enough hours in the day, or days in the
week, to accomplish all of your goals and still have time
for your family, friends, and a little recreation. If you
learn to balance your social life with your academic and
personal commitments, you will discover that you feel
less frenzied and happier.*

*A variety of skills for living can enable you to successfully
handle the challenges of a busy schedule and multiple
responsibilities. From learning to manage your time and
money to earning a driver's license to becoming computer
literate to enjoying the benefits of recreation and leisure,
young women can take control of their lives.*

Time Management

Some people say, "The more you have to do, the more you can do." Managing time is a skill that comes with practice. If you know that you have a busy day ahead, efficiency is important. For example, if you are doing errands, try to do all of the ones in the same neighborhood at the same time so that you can reduce the amount of time you spend traveling to and from various places.

Sometimes you will feel that you are juggling too many responsibilities and that you don't have time to complete them all. If this happens, look objectively at the list of things that you must accomplish and try to rank them in order of priority. When you do this, you will realize that it is okay to put off some of the tasks until sometime in the future.

Sometimes, however, putting off a task is simply a matter of procrastination. If a job, task, or assignment is particularly troublesome, it is easy to rationalize why you should do it later. Unfortunately, "later" always comes and the task is usually even less pleasant and more stress-inducing when you have to do it in a rush. Sometimes it is easier to complete cumbersome tasks or assignments if you break them down into smaller parts, rather than trying to tackle the whole thing at once.

Helpful Hints About Time Management

- *Find your own work pace.* Everyone works at a different pace, some slowly, some in fast bursts of energy. Find what works best for you.

- *Try to accomplish tasks when you are at your best.* For example, are you a morning person or does your energy kick in after lunch?

- *Concentrate.* Things that are done when you concentrate are usually done more thoroughly, skillfully, and effectively than tasks that are done when you are distracted and unfocused. Find the way that you concentrate the best — in a room alone with the door closed; in a library where other people are around; while listening to music.

- *Take breaks.* Avoid "burnout." Know when to stop. Refresh yourself, rest, eat, exercise, or do something else for a while.

- *Avoid clutter.* Clutter can literally make a mess out of things! You will be slowed down if you constantly have to hunt for items you need. Organize your surroundings so that they work for you.

- *Delegate tasks.* Many people feel they have to do everything themselves, and often they exhaust themselves needlessly. Tasks can be more enjoyable and may be accomplished more quickly and effectively when they are shared and delegated.

- *Simplify.* When you are feeling overwhelmed by everything you think you need to do, simplify your life as much as possible. Sometimes you may need to say "no" to tasks and requests and follow some of the time management hints above.

Money Management

It is important to learn to budget your money and not to overspend simply because you would like to have or do something. Some people develop formal budgets where they list their income and then write down each expense they will have for that week or month. If the total output exceeds your income, the budget must be revised.

With your Girl Scout troop or group you probably have had the experience of creating a budget, either for a trip that you wanted to take or for an activity that you were planning. If not, it might be a valuable experience to write a budget for an overnight camping expedition or a party that you would like to have with your friends.

In addition to budgeting, managing money also involves saving. Many teenagers decide to open accounts with their local banks and to deposit some fraction of their income either per week or per month. The amount does not have to be a lot, but if you are consistent in depositing money you will be surprised at how your account will grow.

Lastly, some young women find it helpful to open checking accounts. A checking account can be quite useful because you do not have to carry a lot of cash, you can purchase items by mail, and you can regulate the amount that is being spent each week. It is important to be diligent in recording each check and deposit. Balancing your checkbook against your bank statement once a month is also a good practice.

Find out about money management by organizing a series of "finance clinics." Invite others to attend. Get the "experts" in your community to help — lawyers, insurance agents, stockbrokers, bankers. Just finding out who the experts are will be an education in itself. Any one of these subjects is important to know about and would make a good topic for a finance clinic:

- Advantages and disadvantages of cash buying and credit buying — charge accounts, short-term and long-term installment buying, credit cards, loans.

- Taxes — federal, state, and local — on income, sales, property.

- Investments — stocks, bonds, mutual funds.

Taking to the Road: Earning Your Driver's License

Many people earn a driver's license during their mid- to late teenage years. This is frequently an exciting occurrence because it means growing freedom and independence from adults. Obtaining a driver's license, however, also carries a large measure of responsibility.

Driving safely requires good judgment and mature thought. Good drivers do more than follow the rules. They think and act defensively — always trying to predict what the other drivers around them are likely to do (which may very well include turning when they shouldn't or changing lanes when they haven't signaled).

Consider what you would do in the following situations:

- You are driving at night and the lights of an oncoming car are blinding your vision.

- You get a flat tire as you travel down a main street at rush hour.

- You are driving on the highway and someone in a van deliberately speeds up and bumps your back fender.

- You are ready to leave the football victory celebration party. Your best friend is planning to drive, but you think she has been drinking.

- It's dusk, and you notice a person on the side of the road hitchhiking.

Thirteen states issue restricted juvenile driver's licenses to 14-year-olds.

A car first-aid kit should contain the following:

- Adhesive tape
- Plastic adhesive strips — assorted sizes
- Gauze pads (2 x 2, 3 x 3, 4 x 4)
- Instant chemical ice pack
- Disposable latex gloves (for use in situations involving blood or other body fluids)
- Flashlight
- Plastic bags (for disposal of used materials and for collecting vomitus for analysis)
- Pocket face mask/face shield
- First-aid manual
- Roller gauze bandages (3")
- Pair of good-quality trauma scissors
- Single-use antibacterial wipe for hand
- Cleaning solution or wipe for wounds
- Triangular bandages
- Elastic bandages (3")
- Coins for telephone calls

Young and Dumb

Racing down the highway
Ninety miles an hour
Nothing can stop this feeling
It's a wild kind of power
The lights I see behind me
Colored red white and blue
Are that of a patrolman
Now what am I to do
The exit ramp isn't far away
If I floor it now I can get away
He'll never catch me on 664
I know the road better than
Ever before

So I'll take my chance
Not uttering a word
Dump the clutch
And slam it in third
The engine revving high
At 4000 RPMs
Hoping he won't catch me
If he does — It's the end
The horseshoe-bend curve
Is right up ahead
My steering's gone out . . . . .
Help!!!!!!!!   I'm Dead . . . .

Beth Ann Hacker, 18
Seal of Ohio
Girl Scout Council,
Ohio

Technology Now and in the Future

Do you use a computer to do your homework, keep a diary, draw pictures, play games, or communicate on-line with friends? As we enter the next century, computer literacy is becoming increasingly important. The information highway will enable each of us to communicate and access tremendous amounts of information. Computer technology continues to change with great speed.

On-Line Computing

Studies confirm that participation in computer-based games improves girls' spatial skills.

If your computer at home or at school is connected to a modem, you can use it to receive and exchange information across telephone lines. Using on-line services, you can communicate with teachers, family, or friends through electronic mail or E-mail. You can have E-mail pals all around the world. Bulletin boards allow people to "converse" about specific topics. There is even one devoted to Girl Scouting!

Multimedia

Software applications designed for multimedia mix sound and video with text and graphics. Multimedia personal computers have CD-ROM (compact disk, read-only memory) drives, speakers, or headphones, and a sound board. A variety of creative programs use sound effects and video clips to enhance learning and entertainment.

CD-ROM

CD-ROM disks store information that can be accessed by your computer's CD-ROM drive. A CD-ROM disk can store more than 600 megabytes of information. That's the equivalent of over 300,000 pages in print! Because sound and video take up huge amounts of storage space, a CD-ROM disk is suited to hold this type of information. As technology advances and storage space increases, CD-ROM disks will be able to store entire movies.

Another use for CD-ROM storage is clip art, because graphic files require a tremendous amount of disk space. If you want to include some artwork in a project, you can search through the clip art index in a CD-ROM clip art package until you find the graphic you like. Then you can import or paste the image into your project. Games, dictionaries, encyclopedias, fonts, video clips, and symphonies are other items that can be stored on CD-ROM disks. In the future, a version of *A Resource Book for Senior Girl Scouts* will probably be on CD-ROM!

Interactive CD-ROM

Rather than just using a CD to retrieve stored information, you can use a CD-I (compact disk interactive) to interact with your software. For example, you can enter your height, weight, and pulse rate in a fitness program. The program will monitor the calories you burn as you exercise. Using CD-I, you will be able to take a self-guided tour of a museum, learn to play an instrument, or manipulate the plot in a movie so that you determine the outcome.

Virtual Reality

Images generated by a computer and electronic sensors can give you the sense of taking part in an event such as performing surgery or competing in a high-tech video game. Users of virtual reality technology wear a helmet equipped with tiny video screens directed toward their eyes and use a joy stick or sensor-equipped glove that enables them to manipulate the objects viewed on the screens.

Virtual reality was originally designed as a training tool for astronauts. Today, a surgeon can perform an operation on a virtual body (computerized simulation) of a human. The surgeon can practice various techniques without drawing a drop of blood or making an incision.

This technology has many applications, including engineering, airplane manufacturing, and automotive design. Experts will be able to use virtual reality to simulate a bridge under construction, or the complex wiring in an airplane. Structures or components can be tested in a safe and cost-effective manner without building prototypes. You can even learn to ski on a virtual ski slope. If you fall down, it won't hurt!

Recreation and Leisure

Young women spend their free time in a variety of ways. From team and individual sports to outdoor adventure, from travel to visual arts and music, a wide array of hobbies enrich the lives of teenagers. You can explore any of these interests either alone, with your friends, or through Girl Scouting.

Sports

Participating in sports has many benefits. For example, routine practice sessions or workouts will enhance your physical and psychological well-being. After a period of time, you will discover that your muscles have been strengthened and you will probably also find that you have more, not less, energy after a particularly strenuous workout.

Swinging a bat, jogging a mile, spiking a volleyball, or returning a tennis serve are all good ways to relieve

The Last 7 Seconds

7 seconds left in the game
The away team losing just the same
Down by 2 points, that's all they need
But the home team with too much greed
The shot went up to the away team's joy
The shot was missed, they were destroyed
The home team has just won the game
The away team lost, just the same

Emily K. Baldwin, 14
Penn Lakes Girl Scout Council,
Pennsylvania

SPORTS SAFETY TIPS

Stretch and do warm-up activities for at least ten minutes before starting into the sport.

Take at least a five-minute cooldown period after taking part in the sport (some people will find that their bodies need longer to cool down).

Do not push your body to the extreme.

If something does not feel right, stop and figure out why it does not feel right before going on.

If you are recovering from an injury, do not participate without the approval of a physician.

Remember to keep your body rested.

Wear appropriate safety equipment.

Maintain good nutrition. A well-balanced diet is essential to fuel your body for participation in an activity.

Drink plenty of fluids; water is best.

Protect your body from the harmful rays of the sun; use sunscreen.

Wear appropriate and corre fitted shoes.

Always know how to get h

Dress in layers appropria the climate.

Use good-quality and we fitting equipment.

tensions. On the playing field, the stress that may be present in other areas of your life will be temporarily forgotten. After exercising, you will often find that you have a fresh outlook on life and that you are better equipped to solve problems that may be bothering you.

Playing sports can also enhance your psychological well-being by fostering confidence in your abilities. And if you excel in a particular sport, other people will seek your advice about how to improve their games. In other words, you will have an opportunity to become a leader, to offer support and encouragement to those individuals who do not yet possess your level of expertise. Likewise, athletes are often role models for children and you will be able to set a good example for younger girls to follow.

In fact, you may want to consider volunteering your time to coach a team of younger girls, or working for the Special Olympics in your area. This effort will be especially gratifying because you will not only see other people acquire new athletic skills, but you are also likely to see them mature socially and find a sense of accomplishment in these recreational activities.

With your troop/group or with other older girls from your council, it might be fun to host a day-long sports clinic for Daisy, Brownie, and Junior Girl Scouts. You might consider inviting some professionals working in athletics to this event. You might want to include members of the physical education department from your school in the planning or implementation. The possibilities for a sports clinic are endless, and with a little creativity you and your friends in Girl Scouting can expose the youngsters in your community to the diverse benefits of playing sports.

Girls and women who play sports have higher levels of self-esteem and confidence and lower levels of depression.

High Adventure Programs

Have you ever wanted to climb a mountain, ride the rapids in a raft, or camp out under the stars? If you answered "yes," then you should explore the high adventure programs available in your area. Both Girl Scouting and private organizations offer outdoor experiences that fall into the high adventure category.

For the most part, high adventure activities challenge individuals to confront nature and to overcome their inhibitions about their physical and mental potentials. In most situations, the participants are organized into teams and expected to work as a unit in dealing with the elements, whether they are a steep incline, swift water, wind, snow, or a dark cave. Over the course of the experience, the problems that the teams are required to solve increase in difficulty.

Discussing your reactions to and feelings about your experience is another important part of any high adventure program. Generally, at the conclusion of the activity, teams regroup to share their thoughts about their experiences. Sometimes, participants maintain journals as a way of processing their feelings.

At this point, you may be thinking, "I've never done anything like that before. Can I handle it?" The answer is yes, if you are reasonably physically fit, determined, and willing to try new things. In fact, with the help of adaptive equipment, many of these programs are fully accessible to people with disabilities. Participating in a high adventure program may open many doors for you and reveal that you have a multitude of previously untapped strengths.

The program director at your Girl Scout council office may be able to help you locate high adventure programs. You will also find that many wider opportunities with nationwide participation include aspects of the high adventure process. Resident camps, too, allow young women to try activities such as ropes courses, back country backpacking, canoe trips, and biking expeditions. In

The Hawk

The Hawk flies over country, over sea,
An impersonal watcher on all it sees.

A craggy bluff, with pure white snow,
cold clear currents that take it higher
and higher—
into the waiting clouds of acid rain—
made by the factory below.

A beautiful stream that babbles and
plays by itself,
the pink salmon swirling the water
around a strange blue rock,
that no one knows was put there by
people in orange suits.

Grubby children in the heartland of
America,
playing in the fields where the butter-
flies flit,
and the bugs sprayed with their toxic
pesticides multiply.

People in the cities moving to and fro,
ignoring the feeble stirrings of spring
amongst the steel and concrete
structures
despite the ever present smog and
pollution enveloping the population.

The awesome deep sea fish, and the
whales and dolphins,
majestically surviving in the turbulent
waters,
even though this is where toxic waste
and trash are conveniently dumped.

The Hawk flies over country, over sea,
An impersonal watcher on all it sees.

Tanith Balaban, 17
Girl Scout Council
of Greater St. Louis,
Missouri

addition, many communities have recreational clubs and outings that are available through parks and recreation departments, outdoor stores, and community colleges. The Girl Scout resource *Safety-Wise* is a useful tool for evaluating possible high adventure programs.

Travel

Have you ever wondered what the Coliseum in Rome really looks like? What it really means to speak Greek? What the climate in the Grand Canyon is like? What it would be like to camp out at the state park in a neighboring town? What it is like to visit the big city nearby?

The answers to most of these questions can be found in books or movies or maybe even on your computer network, but perhaps the best way to find the answers is through travel. Taking trips can broaden your horizons by allowing you to meet new people, experience new settings, and learn new skills.

As a Girl Scout, you may already be a seasoned traveler. Perhaps you have attended a national or international wider opportunity with nationwide participation. Maybe you have participated in a regional or local event that involved your council. Or, it might be that your troop/group has organized a variety of trips both large and small, near and far. You might have even journeyed to the Juliette Gordon Low Girl Scout National Center in Savannah, Georgia where many young women attend special programs and view the estate.

- Carry a first-aid kit.

- Carry identification at all times.

- Carry a list of emergency phone numbers and contact people.

- Don't wear your name tag on your uniform.

- Always use the seat belt when traveling in a vehicle.

- Leave a list of participants' names, addresses, and phone numbers with your at-home contact person.

- Follow the procedures set by the council for traveling troops.

- Carry a map of the area where the group will be traveling.

- Leave a trip itinerary with council authorities as required.

- Know how to call for emergency assistance (911, or some other number in your area).

- For each excursion, choose a time and a meeting place for anyone who gets separated from the group.

There are a number of factors to consider when planning to travel with a group of friends. The outline below provides some things to think about as you begin to plan a trip:

- Where will you go?

- What will it cost?

- How will you get there?

- Is there a limit on the number of people who can participate?

- How can you use the services that a travel agent provides?

- Are there cultural issues you should research before you go?

- What should you bring?

This list can help you to begin to consider the many details involved in arranging any type of trip.

The excitement and anticipation involved in planning a trip will help your troop or group to strengthen the bonds of friendship that you have been developing through your other Girl Scout activities. After you choose a destination, each person in the group can work on a different logistical matter so that everyone becomes involved in the project.

How Would You Like to . . .

- Plan a week-long ski trip where everyone enrolls in lessons that are appropriate for her level?

- Plan a hiking trip using the national park system or the youth hostels in your area?

- Plan a theater and shopping trip to a big city that you have always wanted to visit?

- Plan a sailing expedition by chartering a boat for several days?

The Visual Arts

Everywhere you look, you will see evidence of the visual arts. Art is an integral part of your life, whether it occurs in the choreography, stage, or costume design for a play you are in, or the architecture of a building or bridge in the area, or the work that you have done in an art class, or the paintings in your local museum.

Enjoying the arts has a host of benefits. Molding the clay for a sculpture or a pot, painting an intricate picture, capturing a precise moment on film, or visiting a gallery can be immensely gratifying. Participating in artistic activities not only provides an outlet for creative individual expression, but it serves to reduce tensions that may arise in other areas of your life. Art classes, workshops, or seminars are frequently offered in Girl Scout events, after-school programs, community colleges, neighborhood recreation centers, and youth agencies.

Wind

If I were the wind, let me tell you,
I'd have fun, not destroy, that's what I'd do.

I'd blow away rain clouds, let sun shine around,
I'd rush through the treetops with a soft hushing sound.

I'd blow through a bush, I'd rustle some leaves,
I would race through the grain stocks, sheaves upon sheaves.

> *Paula Kinne, 12*
> *Woodland Girl Scout Council,*
> *Wisconsin*

Music

Have you ever stopped to think about the different ways music affects your life, or the ways in which it can be used for self-expression? Because most people enjoy music in some form, it is sometimes considered a universal language. Music, moreover, can help reduce stress, express one's mood, or be a vehicle for celebration.

How many different types of music or instruments are you familiar with? Throughout your life, you will discover that your musical preferences change and grow along with you. For example, the things you might not have cared for as a child might evoke a different response in you now. You might discover that you like melodies, styles, or lyrics that you didn't like previously.

The most frequently sung songs in English are "Happy Birthday to You," "For He's a Jolly Good Fellow," and "Auld Lang Syne."

It might be interesting to compare different contemporary music styles — rhythm and blues, jazz, soul, rock, gospel, salsa, new age, country and western. You are likely to find that in each style there are many variations. Also, try comparing music from different time periods and cultures. What was considered "contemporary music" in seventeenth-century Europe? nineteenth-century America? tenth-century China? or early twentieth-century Africa?

If you're interested in researching music, many places can be helpful to you in your quest. Besides going to museums and music stores, you could go to listening libraries that are stocked with all kinds of recordings. You could also visit music or broadcasting studios, which might give tours to the general public. Some museums and studios also have interactive exhibits that teach visitors about ways to make music — from videos and background film music to compact laser disks and recordings, with over 30 different tracks.

If you have been studying music for a while — long enough to feel confident in your performance abilities — and like the idea of sharing your love for music with others, you might like to teach music. You could gather a small group of interested youngsters or friends to form a music group — a string quartet, a singing/rap group, or any combination of vocal and/or instrumental musicians. Your group could perform in nursing homes, hospitals, day care centers, or senior citizen centers.

Budgeting and saving for the future.

Asserting your opinions and listening to others.

Learning new skills and improving existing ones.

Adhering to a balanced schedule of work and play.

Noting your successes and dealing with your failures.

Cultivating new friendships and maintaining old ones.

Exercising your body and stimulating your mind.

Sample Service Projects

- "Adopt" a park or campground for the summer recreational season under the sponsorship of the managing agency, such as the U.S. Forest Service or your parks and recreation department.

- Help organize and put on a Special Olympics event for your community.

- Help organize a walk or run for Girl Scouts, or help another organization put on such an event.

- Become part of a stream-monitoring program to help ensure clean water for recreation and wildlife.

- Build an exercise course or lay out an orienteering course for others to use.

- Start a chapter of SADD (Students Against Drunk Driving) at your school, or help with a SADD-sponsored activity.

- Volunteer as a scorekeeper, referee, or umpire for a youth sports league.

- Be a member of a choir that performs in nursing homes, hospitals, or schools.

- Help plan and build a community playground. Involve potential users and their families in the process.

- Tutor younger girls in how to use the computer.

- Help count birds during an annual bird-count sponsored by your local Audubon Society.

- Become a guide at a nature center, introducing younger people to the pleasures of the outdoors.

Careers in the Arts, Sports, and Recreation

Coach

Writer

Producer

Fishing guide

Physical education teacher

Illustrator

Music therapist

Architect

Sports journalist

Golf course designer

Sports trainer

Choreographer

Umpire

Radio or television commentator

Recreation director

CHAPTER SIX

Recognitions and Wider Opportunities

Girl Scouting: *Those two simple words mean so many things to so many people. A game of free association with these words might elicit such terms as friends, family, fun, service, career exploration, outdoors, leadership, trips, and personal development, to name only a few. Through the recognitions you choose to earn and the wider opportunities in which you choose to participate, you can tailor the Girl Scout program to meet your own needs.*

Together with the leader of your troop/group — or with the help of another adult from your council — try to explore the many activities outlined in this chapter. As you read about each recognition, you will be able to decide which areas you wish to pursue and which ones will complement work that you have already completed or that you are doing for another reason, such as school or a religious education program. No matter what recognition you choose, you should have fun completing the requirements; after all, that is what Girl Scouting is all about!

Becoming a Campus Girl Scout

By the conclusion of your time as a Senior Girl Scout, you will have acquired an array of experiences and skills. You can continue your Girl Scout career by bridging to the adult level. If you are attending a college, vocational or technical school, or other institute of higher learning, you may join or organize a Campus Girl Scout group through your local council. Young adults, with or without Girl Scout experience, may register as members of a Campus Girl Scout group.

Some activities that Campus Girl Scouts may carry out include: event planning, Girl Scout troop/group sponsorship, program consulting, project management, public relations, troop/group leadership, recruitment activities, fund development, research projects, camping or other outdoor events, and mentoring programs. Campus Girl Scouts wear a special CGS guard with their membership pin.

Over 1,300 young adults are volunteering their talents through Campus Girl Scout groups, established in more than 40 colleges and universities, and the number is growing.

Bridging to Adult Girl Scouting

If you choose to bridge to adult Girl Scouting, you can volunteer your time to your council or directly to girls as a leader of a troop/group. Perhaps you might even want to choose Girl Scouting as a profession. Finally, completing the activities below will enable you to earn the Bridge to Adult Girl Scouts pin.

1. Find out how Girl Scouting is organized in your community.

2. Find out about the volunteer positions that are open to adults.

3. Interview professional Girl Scout staff and find out what kinds of education and experience are needed for key positions.

4. Find out about training available for adults and, if possible, participate in an adult training event.

5. Take on a leadership role in Girl Scouting working with adults. This might be as a Senior Girl Scout Program Aide, a Leader-in-Training, a Counselor-in-Training, a Senior Girl Scout Troop Assistant, an Apprentice Trainer, or a member of an event task group or board committee.

6. Plan or help plan a bridging ceremony, in which you receive your Bridge to Adult Girl Scouts pin. Once you have bridged, you may register as an adult and wear the adult uniform.

The Girl Scout Uniform and Insignia

As a Senior Girl Scout you are entitled, but not required, to wear the Senior Girl Scout uniform. It is a form of identification that shows that you belong to the Girl Scout movement and provides a place to display your recognitions. It is appropriate to wear your uniform to meetings, to special Girl Scout events, when traveling as a troop or individual, or on special Girl Scout days. When a new design is being developed, Senior Girl Scouts from different parts of the country participate in focus groups to offer suggestions and ideas.

Every member of the Girl Scout organization is entitled
to wear the Girl Scouts of the U.S.A. membership pin
and the World Association of Girl Guides and Girl Scouts
(WAGGGS) pin. The three parts of the trefoil that appear
in both pins represent the three parts of the Promise,
something that Girl Scouts and Girl Guides share in a
worldwide sisterhood. Girls in each country wear the
WAGGGS pin along with their own country's pin. The
GSUSA pin comes in two versions, the traditional trefoil
pin or the three faces pin introduced in 1978. The illus-
tration on pages 146–147
will help you determine
where to place your patches
and pins on your uniform.

Recognitions

Much of what you do in your Girl Scout and school activities can help you to earn various recognitions. Note, however, that patches, pins, or badges are only symbols of your work. It is the quality of the experience or product that matters, not the quantity of recognitions obtained.

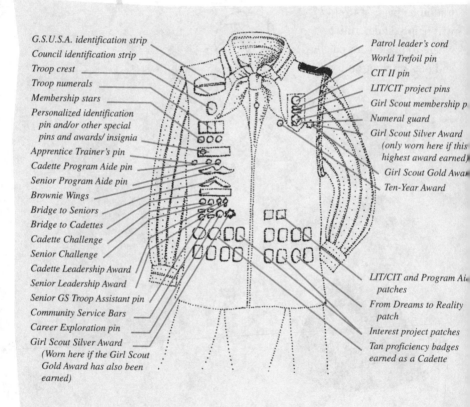

G.S.U.S.A. identification strip
Council identification strip
Troop crest
Troop numerals
Membership stars
Personalized identification
  pin and/or other special
  pins and awards/ insignia
Apprentice Trainer's pin
Cadette Program Aide pin
Senior Program Aide pin
Brownie Wings
Bridge to Seniors
Bridge to Cadettes
Cadette Challenge
Senior Challenge
Cadette Leadership Award
Senior Leadership Award
Senior GS Troop Assistant pin
Community Service Bars
Career Exploration pin
Girl Scout Silver Award
  (Worn here if the Girl Scout
  Gold Award has also been
  earned)

Patrol leader's cord
World Trefoil pin
CIT II pin
LIT/CIT project pins
Girl Scout membership p
Numeral guard
Girl Scout Silver Award
  (only worn here if this
  highest award earned)
Girl Scout Gold Awa
Ten-Year Award

LIT/CIT and Program Ai
  patches
From Dreams to Reality
  patch
Interest project patches
Tan proficiency badges
  earned as a Cadette

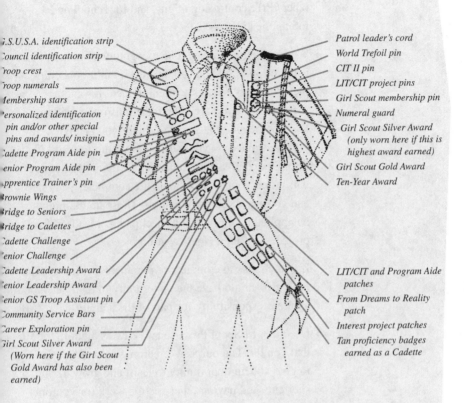

U.S.A. identification strip
Council identification strip
Troop crest
Troop numerals
Membership stars
Personalized identification
    pin and/or other special
    pins and awards/ insignia
Cadette Program Aide pin
Senior Program Aide pin
Apprentice Trainer's pin
Brownie Wings
Bridge to Seniors
Bridge to Cadettes
Cadette Challenge
Senior Challenge
Cadette Leadership Award
Senior Leadership Award
Senior GS Troop Assistant pin
Community Service Bars
Career Exploration pin
Girl Scout Silver Award
    (Worn here if the Girl Scout
    Gold Award has also been
    earned)

Patrol leader's cord
World Trefoil pin
CIT II pin
LIT/CIT project pins
Girl Scout membership pin
Numeral guard
Girl Scout Silver Award
    (only worn here if this is
    highest award earned)
Girl Scout Gold Award
Ten-Year Award

LIT/CIT and Program Aide
    patches
From Dreams to Reality
    patch
Interest project patches
Tan proficiency badges
    earned as a Cadette

General Guidelines for All Recognitions

1. Work with an adult. It won't always be the same
   person — adviser, program consultant, project director,
   council staff, or mentor. The adult will give you
   guidance and sign off on the completed requirements,
   but the work should be yours.

2. Keep a record of your work. This can be useful for other Girl Scout recognitions, and for school and job applications.

3. Work done to complete one recognition should not be used for another. You can, however, build on a completed activity to satisfy a requirement for another recognition if you are able to demonstrate additional learning beyond the scope of the original activity. Say you are trained by your science museum to lead kids through exhibits, and you earn a Community Service bar. When your service hours are complete, you plan and construct your own exhibit. Those hours might be applied to an interest project patch, a leadership project, or even a Gold Award project.

4. If you choose to complete requirements with a group, each girl should have the opportunity to plan, lead, and assume responsibility for part of the activity.

5. Use the Girl Scout Promise and Law as a guide for all that you do. The purpose of earning recognitions is to give you an opportunity to learn and grow. Using shortcuts and having others do the work for you only defeat that purpose.

6. Always consult *Safety-Wise* when planning an event or wider opportunity, or when working with people outside of Girl Scouting.

Interest Projects

Most interest projects have components relating to career exploration, skill development, and service. You may choose to do them by yourself or with others. You may decide to work on a project that is described in the book *Cadette and Senior Girl Scout Interest Projects*, or you may decide to design your own project based on the prescribed general guidelines. Whatever route you choose, seek an adviser who is well versed in the subject area you wish to explore.

Senior Girl Scout Community Service Bar

Two steps are involved in earning the Senior Girl Scout Community Service bar. First, you must select the organization in which you would like to work, and people there must agree to train you for a minimum of four hours. Your council must approve both the organization you have selected and the training that they propose.

You may check with your council or service unit for training programs that have been approved, or you can do your own research on organizations that may offer opportunities, and then get council approval. It may be harder for you individually to find organizations that will train and make volunteer time available. Therefore, it is recommended that you approach organizations as a group with a supervising adult who is a Girl Scout.

Second, you must commit yourself to a minimum of 25 hours of service to an organization. Furthermore, if you choose to volunteer at least 25 hours to the Girl Scout organization, you can receive the Community Service bar in Girl Scouting. For example, you might volunteer your time at a special event for younger girls, write for an older girl newsletter, or help with special projects at the council office.

Recognitions for Leadership

Leadership Projects

GSUSA leadership projects present an opportunity for Senior Girl Scouts to take the lead with activities involving younger girls. As a Senior Girl Scout you are very capable of making contributions; however, because you are not yet an adult, you cannot be left alone with a group of girls. An adult must be present at all times for liability reasons.

In choosing a leadership project, you may be a Senior Girl Scout Program Aide, a Leader-in-Training, a Senior Girl Scout Troop Assistant, a Counselor-in-Training, or a Counselor-in-Training II.

• *Senior Girl Scout Program Aide*

Pin. Received after completion of training.
Patch. Received after completion of service hours.
For a detailed description of this opportunity, see pages 72–73 in the chapter on leadership.

• *Leader-in-Training*
Pin. Received after completion of training.
Patch. Received after completion of internship.
More complete information on the Leader-in-Training
recognition can be found on page 73.

• *Senior Girl Scout Troop Assistant*
Pin. Received after completion of one-year service to a
troop or group. See page 73 for more information.

• *Counselor-in-Training*
Pin. Received after completion of training.
Patch. Received after completion of the internship.
A thorough discussion of the Counselor-in-Training
option can be found on page 74 in this handbook.

• *Counselor-in-Training II (CIT II)*
Pin. A pin, different from the one you get for participation in the CIT project, will be received after completion
of the training and internship. More details about the CIT
II project can be found on page 74 of this handbook.

Senior Girl Scout Leadership Award
In working toward the Senior Girl Scout Leadership
Award, you build on your previous leadership experi-
ence. To earn this recognition, do the following:

Start by reading Chapter Three on leadership. Log at
least 30 hours in two or more of the following activities.
If you spend 30 or more hours on only one of the options

below, you must still work on a second activity option for a minimum of three hours. The experiences may be in or outside of Girl Scouting.

- Serve a term as an officer in a group (for example, president or treasurer).

- Assist in the leadership of a group engaged in Girl Scout activities.

- Plan and give a public presentation (see Chapter Four).

- Serve in a leadership capacity for your council (for example, member of a wider opportunities committee).

- Work with an adult who is in a leadership position in the community (for example, director of the town planning board or director of a social service agency).

Evaluate your experience with your adviser or another adult: What did you learn? What skills do you still need to build? What is your personal style of leadership?

The Career Exploration Pin

To earn the Career Exploration pin, you must complete the first two requirements below and at least one of the suggested options. Options can be individual or group projects.

1. Read the discussion of careers in Chapter 4.

2. Write your own résumé. See pages 101–103 for assistance.

Option 1: Plan a Career Fair

Bring people and careers together to meet a need in your community.

- Decide on your audience.

- Compile a list of organizations and businesses that you would like to see represented.

- Develop a strategy for identifying and contacting people — calling, writing, faxing.

- Find a place to hold the fair, check calendars, and set a date.

- Identify all essential tasks and responsibilities and those people who will follow through on them.

- Publicize the fair to your intended audience.

- Afterwards, evaluate the fair — what could have been improved, what did you learn?

- Thank those who helped.

Option 2: Plan a Trip to Explore Careers

This is an opportunity to go where the careers or career training can be found. Your travels can lead you to the workplace, training facilities, or colleges.

- Identify the career or career areas you would like to focus on.

- Brainstorm a list of potential places to visit — use business directories, newspapers, phone books, and career resources.

- Decide on your time commitment — how many trips will you make, or will there be one trip with multiple stops?

- List places and potential speakers. If necessary, develop a budget for what you want to do and plan how you will pay for it.

- Develop your plan and itinerary — arrange for all necessary things, such as scheduling, transportation, food, and lodging.

- Research the careers and places you will be visiting.

- Carry out your plan. (Don't forget to review *Safety-Wise*!)

- Evaluate — discuss what you learned and how you might do things differently.

- Thank appropriate people with letters.

Option 3: Carry Out a Career Internship
This is an opportunity to go beyond reading and to mentor with someone who is in a career that truly interests you.

Here are some hints:

- Make a list of possible careers that you are interested in, then research and rank your choices.

- Look for a possible mentor. Your council might help you by suggesting someone, or you can pick a mentor yourself and clear the placement with your adviser and the council.

- When you have identified the possibilities, approach the one that looks best for you. You may go through a human resources department in a large organization, speak directly to an individual whom you want as a mentor, or work with a person whose job is to match young people with adult mentors.

- Be prepared to answer questions about your interests, why you want to intern, and how much time you can spend doing it. (You might do it during a school break, after school, or on weekends.)

- When you connect with a mentor, spend some time discussing expectations that you both have for the experience. This will include time commitments, opportunities for job shadowing, actual work expectations, and possibly tips on dress and conduct.

- An internship is what you make of it. Work with your mentor to find out about training for a particular job, what typical workday activities are, what other jobs are available in the field, and what the future is expected to be for the job. Identify professional organizations associated with the job and find out about possible paid internship or apprentice positions for high school graduates.

- Decide how you will evaluate your internship.

- Keep a journal of your experience.

Option 4: Get a Paying Job

Getting a job after school, on weekends, or over a school holiday that pays money can be a valuable experience for a teenager. Even if you are working in a capacity that will not become a future career, you are still acquiring important skills.

- Read the section on pages 103–105 about job interviews.

- Interview for a job, taking your résumé with you or sending it in beforehand. Decide in advance what skills you have that will be important for the job so that you can address them in your interview.

- If you do not get a job on your first try, determine what you might do differently in your next interview. (You might even speak to the person who interviewed you to ask for suggestions.)

- Once you have a job, keep a journal about what you learn about work and your personal work habits for a period of time. Evaluate your experience with your adviser.

Option 5: Start Your Own Business

Here's an opportunity to learn about entrepreneurship. Ideally, your adviser for this project will be an individual who is knowledgeable about the business world — perhaps a current or retired business owner, someone from a professional women's organization, or a school business club adviser.

Here's a brief outline of how to set up a business:

1. Identify a need.

2. Determine how to fill the need through a service to be performed or the development of a product.

3. Plan and implement business operations:

a. Find out about laws that will affect you (insurance, liability, tax).

b. Develop a time line for project implementation.

c. Develop a budget.

d. Obtain money to buy supplies.

e. Set up facilities.

f. Obtain supplies and materials.

g. Plan production methods.

h. Set a price.

i. Produce the object (if a product-oriented business).

j. Advertise and market the service or product.

k. Implement accounting procedures; keep records.

4. Determine how profits will be used.

5. Evaluate your operations and improve them where needed.

This Challenge asks you to put the Girl Scout Promise and Law into action. When you combine your talents and energies with your values and convictions, you can make a positive difference in the lives of others. You can work on the activities alone or with others who share your interests.

Section 1: Developing Your Potential
Challenge: Design a self-development plan.

- Set some short-term (one week to one year) and long-term (five to ten years) goals for yourself in the following areas:

Education	Work
Friends	Family
Health	Recreation

- Prioritize your goals and develop a time line for your short-term goals.

- Decide what kinds of skills might help you achieve your long-range goals and how you might acquire those skills.

- Follow through on your plan for a period of at least two months. At the end of this time, evaluate your progress and your time lines. What have you learned?

Section 2: Relating to Others
Challenge: Examine your skills in relating to others.

- Plan to increase your skills in at least one area of relating—family, friends, peers, children, adults.

Write out personal goals to do this. Develop a time line that includes skill development (such as practicing, reading articles, or attending workshops) and planned experiences in relating to others.

- With another person, evaluate what you learned about yourself from identifying your goals and working toward them.

Section 3: Developing Values for Living
Challenge: Decide on what you value the most.

- What issues or concerns are most important to you? List ten things that you would most like to change and how. Circle those things that you can begin to work on right now.

- Decide how the Promise and Law can help you achieve positive change. Decide on at least three activities that you can and will do to make a positive change for yourself and others. If you work with others, be able to distinguish your own personal contributions to the effort.

- Find a way to summarize your discoveries about yourself and your values.

- What activities did you complete? Did you learn things about yourself after working on each one?

- Is there a difference between what you actually say and do and what you believe? How can you work to change this?

Section 4: Contributing to Society

Challenge: Participate in a service project that will benefit something you value in your community in some way.
You may join an effort directed by others, or you may
design, develop, and carry out your own effort. You can
work alone or with others, but be sure you choose an
activity that is personally important. There are ideas for
service projects in every chapter. Your effort should total
a minimum of 15 hours. When the project is complete,
consider the following:

• Who or what benefited from this service project?
  How?

• Which of your talents were put to use?

• What skills and abilities would you like to develop
  further?

• What did you learn about yourself and your values?

Section 5: Helping Others Know About Girl Scouting

Challenge: Get involved in Girl Scouting beyond your
troop/group. You may select an activity from the ones
listed or develop your own plan to help others know
about Girl Scouting.

• Serve on a councilwide girl planning group.

• Help plan a Cadette or Senior Girl Scout conference,
  Thinking Day event, or other special event.

• Serve on the council board or a committee or task
  group in your council.

• Help with a council-sponsored training event for adults.

- Conduct tours of council properties or facilities.

- Help with a community task force to extend Girl Scouting to girls in an underserved area.

After you have completed the five challenges in this recognition, use the questions below to help you and your leader evaluate your experience.

1. What have you discovered about the world of Girl Scouting?

2. In what situations have you demonstrated a real under-standing of the Promise and the Law by applying them to everyday living?

3. How has your project benefited others?

4. What are some possible ways that you could continue to show your concern in this area in the future?

5. In what ways have you shown that you are capable of self-direction? In what ways were you able to work, plan, and share with a group?

6. What other things have you learned about yourself?

7. How have you demonstrated what you value?

Religious recognitions have been developed nationally by individual religious groups so that a girl might learn more about her own faith and become a stronger member of her religious group. Use the chart below to contact your group at the national level, and work with your clergy or youth adviser to pursue the recognition in your community.

Sources of Information About Religious Recognitions

Bahai
Unity of Mankind, Bahai's Committee on Scouting, Bahai National Center, Wilmette, IL 60091, (708) 869-9039

Buddhist
Padma Award, Ages 15–17
Buddhist Church of America, National Headquarters, 1710 Octavia Street, San Francisco, CA 94109, (415) 776-5600

Christian Science
P.R.A.Y., P.O. Box 6900, St. Louis, MO 63123, (800) 933-7729

Eastern Orthodox
Alpha Omega, Ages 15–17
P.R.A.Y., P.O. Box 6900, St. Louis, MO 63123, (800) 933-7729

Episcopal
God and Life, Ages 15–17, Grades 10–12
P.R.A.Y., P.O. Box 6900, St. Louis, MO 63123, (800) 933-7729

Hindu
North American Hindu Association,
46133 Amesbury Drive, Plymouth, MI 48170,
(313) 459-5059 or 981-2323

Islamic
Muslimeen Award, Ages 15–17
Islamic Committee on Girl Scouting,
31 Marian Street, Stamford, CT 06907, (203) 359-3593

Jewish
Menorah Award, Ages 15–17
National Jewish Girl Scout Committee of the Synagogue
Council of America, 327 Lexington Avenue, New York,
NY 10016, (212) 686-8670

Lutheran
Lutheran Living Faith, Ages 14–17, Grades 9–12
P.R.A.Y., P.O. Box 6900, St. Louis, MO 63123,
(800) 933-7729

(Mormon) Church of Jesus Christ of Latter-day Saints
Young Woman of Promise, Ages 14–15;
Young Woman of Faith, Young Womanhood Recognition,
Ages 16–17
Salt Lake District Center,
Church of Jesus Christ of Latter-day Saints,
Salt Lake City, UT 84104,
(801) 240-2141

Protestant and Independent Christian Churches
God and Life, Ages 14–17, Grades 9–12
P.R.A.Y., P.O. Box 6900, St. Louis, MO 63123,
(800) 933-7729

(Quakers) Society of Friends
Spirit of Truth, Ages 14–17, Grades 10–12
Friends Committee on Scouting, c/o Dennis Clarke,
85 Willowbrook Road, Cromwell, CT 06416,
(203) 635-1706

Reorganized Church of Jesus Christ of Latter-day Saints
Exploring My Life and World, Ages 15–17
Youth Ministries Office, The Auditorium, P.O. Box 1059,
Independence, MO 64051, (816) 833-1000

Roman Catholic Church
Marian Medal, Age 15, Spirit Alive, Ages 15-17
National Federation for Catholic Youth Ministry,
3700-A Oakview Terrace, NE, Washington, DC 20017,
Att.: Orders Clerk, (202) 636-3825

Unitarian Universalist
Religion in My Life, Ages 15–17
Unitarian Universalist, 25 Beacon Street, Boston, MA
02108, (617) 742-2100

Unity Church
Association of Unity Churches,
P.O. Box 610, Lee's Summit, MO 64063, (816) 524-7414

The American Indian Youth Award Certificate

You may earn the American Indian Youth Award Certificate as a registered Girl Scout. Your adviser should be someone other than your parent or guardian. You may use the tribe of your own heritage, or the tribe of the community in which you live, to fulfill the following requirements:

• Have full tribal dress; make part of it.

• Do and explain two traditional dances.

• Sing two American Indian songs, recite an American Indian prayer, or speak the language of your tribe.

• Make, show, and explain a craft from the tribe.

• Develop knowledge of the tribe.

Request a certificate form from your council or from Girl Scouts of the U.S.A., Membership and Program Cluster, 420 Fifth Avenue, New York, N.Y. 10018-2702. The form should be completed by you and signed by your adviser or leader. A related recognition is the American Indian Youth Award Silver Medallion. This recognition is awarded annually to one girl and one boy of American Indian descent who have met the requirements for the certificate and won the competition at the American Indian Girl Scouting/Boy Scouting Seminar.

Ten-Year Pin

If you have been a Girl Scout for ten years prior to age 18, you are entitled to wear the Ten-Year Award. (These years do not have to be continuous.)

Macy Lamp Pin

If you attend an official GSUSA event or training session at Edith Macy Conference Center in Briarcliff Manor, New York, you may join a long line of women who wear the Macy Lamp pin. It signifies the special learning that takes place while you are there and is presented in a ceremony at Macy.

Juliette Low World Friendship Pin

This pin is given to any girl or adult who participates in a wider opportunity sponsored by the Juliette Gordon Low World Friendship Fund. You may travel abroad to a WAGGGS-sponsored event, or represent GSUSA at an international event within the United States. The pins are presented by GSUSA.

Lifesaving Awards

The Bronze Cross and the Medal of Honor are two very special awards that have been a part of the Girl Scout program since the start of the movement. Your Girl Scout council documents specific actions that have led to a person saving a life or attempting to save a life, with national awards determined by GSUSA. Additional information is available in *Safety-Wise* and through your council office.

The Girl Scout Gold Award, the highest achievement in Girl Scouting, has five requirements, all of which demand efficient organizational, time management, and leadership skills. The requirements are:

1. Earn four interest project patches on topics related to your Gold Award project. See *Cadette and Senior Girl Scout Interest Projects.*

2. Earn the Career Exploration pin (for details, see pages 152–156).

3. Earn the Senior Girl Scout Leadership Award (for details, see pages 151–152).

4. Earn the Senior Girl Scout Challenge (for details, see pages 158–161).

5. Plan and implement a Girl Scout Gold Award project that requires at least 50 hours of work (see pages 169–173).

Requirements 1–4 may be completed in any order, but must be fulfilled prior to beginning the Gold Award project. Note that your accomplishments prior to registration as a Senior Girl Scout may not be used toward the completion of your Gold Award.

About 2,500 young women, or 6 percent of Senior Girl Scouts, earn Gold Awards each year.

The Girl Scout Gold Award

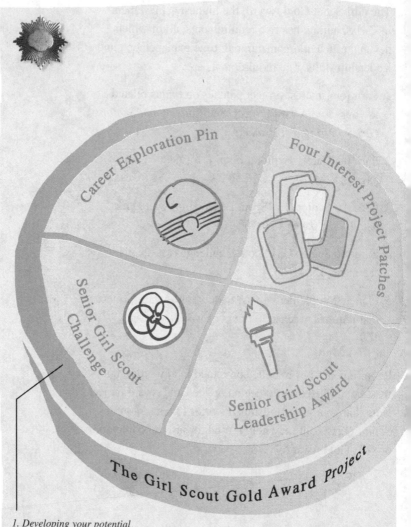

Career Exploration Pin

Four Interest Project Patches

Senior Girl Scout Challenge

Senior Girl Scout Leadership Award

The Girl Scout Gold Award *Project*

1. *Developing your potential*
2. *Relating to others*
3. *Developing values for living*
4. *Contributing to society*
5. *Helping others know about Girl Scouts*

The Girl Scout Gold Award Project

A Gold Award project is an opportunity for you to put your leadership skills, career interests, and personal values together to serve your community. You may plan your project individually or you may choose to work with other Girl Scouts. If you choose to engage in a collective project, each member of the team must adopt equal amounts of responsibility, and everyone must be given an opportunity to learn and grow by acquiring the skills needed to accomplish the project goals. Your project should expand upon the skills that you have gained by completing the first four requirements.

Here are some basic guidelines:

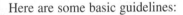

- Your project should meet an expressed need in the community. Community service is always done without expectation of payment or reward.

- You are encouraged to go beyond the Girl Scouting community. If the project involves Girl Scouts, some segment of the project plan must include the outlying community. (For example, if you plan to develop a nature trail on council property, you might consult with community resources, involve volunteers from a service club, and develop a brochure for outside groups.)

- You must select a project adviser/consultant. Your council or troop adviser can assist you with this process if you need help. If this role is filled by your troop adviser or parent/guardian, you must seek guidance from a content expert for at least a part of your project (for example, input from a law enforcement official for a project involving self-defense techniques).

- You may enlist others to help you, or work through organizations to put your project in place, but it is your vision and leadership that should make it happen.

- You must consider at the outset what funding is necessary to successfully execute the project. Create a realistic budget that does not rely on securing grants or raising large sums of money. Remember that you cannot collect money for other organizations; however, you can ask for goods and services. Any fund raising or solicitation of materials needs to be approved by your council.

- Your project should take a time commitment of 50 hours, at the minimum. Keep a log of your hours to share with your project adviser. This time includes planning, making contacts, training others, and actually implementing the project.

- If your project is to become ongoing, such as a suicide hotline for teens or an interpretive nature trail, plan how it can be sustained or maintained.

- Always check *Safety-Wise* when planning your project. If you are proposing to address "sensitive issues" as defined in *Safety-Wise*, you will need to follow GSUSA and council guidelines for Girl Scout involvement and have council permission before beginning.

It is best to run the idea by your adviser first. While some ideas may seem appropriate "on paper," when you begin to assess the actual time commitment or long-term ramifications you may realize that your proposal needs to be more fully researched and planned. For example, you may decide to work with senior citizens by baking cookies for them and spending an afternoon visiting with them. In this form, the project is too simplistic, but the underlying premise is a good one.

To make this project worthy of the Girl Scout Gold Award, you could expand the process to include working with the recreation staff of a nursing home or senior center to develop ways in which the residents could be included in the baking of cakes or cookies. Participants could be asked to bring in their favorite recipes, which could later be compiled into a cookbook. The home or center might then sell the cookbook and use the profits for establishing ongoing cooking lessons.

The Girl Scout Gold Award Application

Every Senior Girl Scout who would like to earn a Gold Award must complete and submit an application to her council at least six weeks prior to the date that she proposes to begin her project. You can obtain all the necessary forms and information from your council office.

The application is comprised of three parts. The first asks for personal data like your name, address, and phone number. In the second section you must list the interest project patches you earned, the career exploration option that you completed, your Senior Girl Scout Leadership Award activities, and the details of your Senior Girl Scout Challenge. The third part requires you to write brief answers to a series of seven questions regarding the specifics of your interests and your project.

In preparing a Gold Award application, you will need to develop a plan and create a time line for yourself. Be sure to consider the points in the checklist on pages 169–170.

When you have completed your application, read it! Check carefully for spelling and grammatical errors. Ask your troop members or someone whose judgment you respect the following questions:

- Will someone who does not know who I am understand *what* I want to accomplish?

- Will she or he understand *why* I chose this project?

- Will she or he understand *how* I plan to meet my intended goals?

Once your application is complete, you must submit it to the Girl Scout council office at least six weeks before you plan to begin the initial project steps. Individuals at the council (in most cases, a special Girl Scout Gold Award advisory committee) will review your proposal and may make suggestions regarding your project. They may suggest adjustments in your plan based on their experience with other projects, or assign an adviser to work with you. The council may advise you that your proposal does not meet the standards outlined in this chapter. For example, it may be in violation of *Safety-Wise*, or it may be in conflict with Girl Scout program standards. The time requirements or substance of the project may not be in keeping with the 50-hour minimum or the individual commitment required. You should receive some response from the council within six weeks. If you have not received any word after three weeks, send a follow-up letter or make a phone call.

Note: Do not begin any work on your project until you have received notification from your council.

The Girl Scout Gold Award Final Report
When you have completed all the activities related to your
Gold Award project, you will be required to submit a final
report to your council. This form is comprised of two
parts: Section 1 asks for personal data such as your name,
address, and phone number. The second section asks you
to write short essays about the outcomes of your project.

When the Paperwork Is Done
When your council has approved your final report, your
name will be forwarded to GSUSA national headquarters
and you will receive a letter of congratulations and a
certificate from the GSUSA National President. You
can also receive recognition from the President of the
United States. Ask your leader or Girl Scout council for
more details.

Many councils arrange for special Gold Award ceremonies. A wide variety of procedures are used. The book
Ceremonies in Girl Scouting has an example of a Gold
Award ceremony. It should be a time of honoring your
accomplishments and thanking the individuals who have
helped you along the way.

By receiving a Gold Award, you become a member of a
special group of women who, throughout the history of
Girl Scouting, have received the highest recognition in
the organization. In Juliette Low's day, the highest award
was the Golden Eaglet. By earning the Gold Award of
today, you will be recognized by your community as
someone who is capable and competent. You will, moreover, be eligible for certain scholarships available only to
Gold Award recipients. Contact your council for a listing
of institutions that offer these scholarships.

Wider Opportunities

Wider opportunities with nationwide participation have been held for over 50 years at the national and international levels for girls 12–18 years of age.

Has your troop or group ever gone on a trip? Camping for a weekend? To the local college for a seminar? To the park for a picnic? Each one of these activities can be labeled a wider opportunity. In the broadest sense, the term "wider opportunity" means any activity beyond the routine troop or group setting. Sometimes confusion arises because girls think that wider opportunities are simply those events that are listed in the *Wider Ops* magazine. To eliminate this confusion, the events described in the magazine will be called "wider opportunities with nationwide participation."

Opportunities

Girl Scouts is a wider opportunity.
With growing support
from our community,
All Girl Scouts will continue to grow
And the benefits we all will show

Maturity
Generosity
Optimism
And Strength

Wider Opportunities with Nationwide Participation

For many young women, attending a wider opportunity with nationwide participation is a highlight of their career in Girl Scouting. Here are some important points to keep in mind about these particular events:

- Ask for help with your application. Parents, Girl Scout leaders, teachers, and friends are all good sources of inspiration, and they may be able to offer you constructive criticism. They also may be able to remind you about skills or experiences that you have not addressed in your application.

We learn and have fun in the rain or the sun,
Play a game or sing a song,
We all have a place to belong.

Bring a friend, maybe two
There is always something new to do.

Sleep under the stars, sing in the rain,
cook in a box, we have everything to gain.
Hike in the woods or bake a cake,
Scale a wall or swim in a lake.

In the Girl Scouts there is nothing we can't do,
All we need is the chance to try.
So dressed in our green and blue,
Our dreams soar beyond the sky.

We are becoming well-rounded
It's for this reason that Girl Scouts was founded.

The wider opportunity we have received,
And together we will succeed!

> *Monica S. Knapp, 16*
> *Kickapoo Council of Girl Scouts, Illinois*

- When writing your application, be very specific about your skills and accomplishments. Relate those things that you have done to the event requirements described in the magazine.

- Do not allow the cost of a wider opportunity with nationwide participation to deter you from applying. You may be eligible for scholarship money through either your council, GSUSA, or a private organization. Also, you may want to consider baby-sitting, hosting a garage sale, walking dogs, or other jobs in your community as a means to earn some of the money necessary to attend an event.

- Be aware that the selection process is highly competitive. Each year, many more girls apply than the number of openings can accommodate.

- If you are not selected one year, apply again the next. Perseverance and determination are important qualities for whatever endeavors you choose to pursue throughout your life.

If you are accepted to a wider opportunity with nationwide participation, try to work closely with your council and the sponsoring council to be sure that all the necessary forms and payments are submitted in a timely fashion. See *Wider Ops* magazine, published annually, for more detailed information.

Researching the area that you will be visiting will also enrich your trip. If you decide to take "SWAPS," or mementos, try to be creative. Give something that is inexpensive yet conveys something about yourself and the area where you live.

Other Wider Opportunities

If you are not selected for a wider opportunity with nationwide participation, don't despair. You can still travel as a Girl Scout. Some ideas that you might want to consider are the following:

Plan Your Own Trip
Gather a group of your friends and your leader and plan a visit to a place that you have always wanted to go. See Chapter Five for more information and ideas about planning trips. You might even consider an international journey that includes a stay at one of the world centers. For more information on these facilities, see pages 5–6.

Use the GSUSA Trekking Network
GSUSA publishes a resource, the *Trekking Network Directory*, that lists councils willing to provide inexpensive accommodations for traveling Girl Scout troops or groups. This resource also lists Counselor-in-Training opportunities and camp sessions open to out-of-council applicants. To obtain this information, contact your council.

Realizing potential

Exploring careers

Creating service projects

Organizing and leading groups

Going new places and doing new things

Nurturing skills

Implementing new strategies

Teaching younger girls new skills

Initiating positive change

Opening doors to the future

Narrating stories

Sharing experiences with others

Sample Gold Award Projects

- Work with people in your community government to develop a recreational bicycle route.

- Involve your community in an endeavor to clean up a polluted area.

- Organize a fair to help people identify volunteer opportunities in the community. Create a directory of organizations that use volunteers.

- Start a group at school for victims of violence, after recruiting qualified adults to assist as advisers.

- Write and produce a play that causes people to think about a community problem and to change either themselves or their surroundings to solve the problem.

- Help organize and sponsor a historical walking tour around the community, using checkpoints and an interpretive map.

- Create and implement an erosion prevention plan for a favorite park or hiking trail, with help from a soil conservation agency.

- Plan and coordinate a community or school event that celebrates different cultures through art, dance, song, costume, and food.

- Organize a drive to collect used radios, and establish a place where the homeless can obtain free radios, batteries, and headsets.

Careers In Travel

Travel agent

Pilot

Cruise director

Flight attendant

Air traffic controller

Ambassador

Translator

Tour guide

International program coordinator

International news correspondent

Professor

International banker

International health educator

Naval officer

Red Cross nurse

Index

Special acknowledgement is given to Tanith Balaban,
Emily Baldwin, Bea Barber, Shaunda Betts, Karin Brereton,
Dishile Davis, Debbie Folz, Beth Ann Hacker, Paula Kinne,
Monica S. Knapp, Dana Latimer, Joanne Payne, Jameika
Sampson, Sarah Sellers, Cara Tirone and Angela Twining for
allowing us to print their poetry.

GSUSA also expresses appreciation for the hundreds of poems
that we received from Girl Scouts all around the country.

The attributed poetry and quotations that appear in this handbook were submitted by Girl Scout members as original work.
GSUSA claims no responsibility for the origin of this material.